The Secret of Life: Development of the Spiritual Consciousness

Sorocaima Salerno

The Secret of Life: Development of the Spiritual Consciousness
Copyright © 2021 by Sorocaima Salerno

Library of Congress Control Number: 2021915940
ISBN-13: Paperback: 978-1-64749-524-4
         ePub: 978-1-64749-525-1

All rights reserved. No part of this publication may be reproduced, distributed, or transmitted in any form or by any means, including photocopying, recording, or other electronic or mechanical methods, without the prior written permission of the publisher or author, except in the case of brief quotations embodied in critical reviews and certain other noncommercial uses permitted by copyright law.

Although every precaution has been taken to verify the accuracy of the information contained herein, the author and publisher assume no responsibility for any errors or omissions. No liability is assumed for damages that may result from the use of information contained within.

Printed in the United States of America

GoToPublish LLC
1-888-337-1724
www.gotopublish.com
info@gotopublish.com

This book is dedicated
to my wife Alba Salerno, who endured many hours of isolation to produce it.
And to all people who question the meaning of this human life
and seek answers that they cannot find in religion.
For others, their time has not yet come.
But this is your time, and you have been led to this moment.

ACKNOWLEDGEMENTS

To all the mystics who have passed through this world and whose revelations and spiritual light have allowed humanity to reach a higher level of consciousness. Especially, to the two greatest who have attained perfect union with God: Gautama the Buddha and Jesus Christ.

I am particularly grateful to Swami Vivekananda, one of the most enlightened spiritual leaders of the 19th century. And most especially, I owe my thanks to Joel Goldsmith, the most enlightened mystic in the Western world in the 20th century.

I also want to thank my dear granddaughters Isabella, Gabriela and Sofia for editing the English translation I made of my book in Spanish "El Secreto de la Vida - Desarrollo de la Conciencia Espiritual", and a few new additions to the book.

CONTENTS

Introduction to the second edition xi
Introduction to the first edition xvii
Chapter 1   The Spiritual Sense 1
      1.1 Journey to our inner world 1
      1.2 Three levels of consciousness 2
      1.3 How to get to know God 3
      1.4 The fable of Mount Olympus 5
      1.5 Our true identity 6
      1.6 The parable of the Prodigal Son 8
      1.7 Human beings are "walking dead" 9
      1.8 Spiritual life 10
      1.9 Developing a spiritual awareness 12
      1.10 The concept of pre-existence 13
      1.11 The most important commandment 16
      1.12 Love your neighbor 18
      1.13 The law of forgiveness 19
      1.14 Spiritual power is absolute 20
      1.15 The secret of your security: "pray without ceasing" 21
Chapter 2   God 27
      2.1 False Concepts about God 27
      2.2 Karma or Law of Cause and Effect 30

  2.3 Thoughts are Actions 32
  2.5 What is the best religion? 36
  2.6 God is an experience, not a belief 39
Chapter 3 God and His Creation 43
  3.1 The Mystery of Genesis 43
  3.2 Spiritual Consciousness or God 44
  3.3 The Origen of the Universe 46
  3.4 Consciousness is only one 47
  3.5 Consciousness is what we are 49
  3.6 You are Consciousness 51
  3.7 You are Realized Consciousness 52
  3.8 Your level of Realized Consciousness determines the quality of your existence. 54
  3.9 Consciousness after Death 58
  3.10 Questions and Answers 60
  3.11 All things were made by God 63
  3.12 All good things come to us from God 64
  3.13 God Created a Spiritual Universe 66
Chapter 4 Man and his creation 69
  4.1 Mental creation 69
  4.2 Our five senses and our mind deceive us 73
  4.3 Do not Judge by Appearances 75
  4.4 Control your Mind and your Thoughts ... 77
  4.5 Levels of a Single Consciousness 79
  4.6 Mental Awareness and the Subconscious 81
  4.7 The Universal Hypnotism 83
  4.8 Evil is not personalized 85
  4.9 Spiritual Healing 87
  4.10 Detachment from the Things of this World 89

    4.11 God is our Provider 91
    4.12 The Mind and its Power 94
    4.13 A personal God that does not exist 100
    4.14 God does not participate in human affairs 102
    4.15 The Third and Fourth Dimension 105
    4.16 Quantum physics and mysticism 107
    4.17 Recapitulation 108
Chapter 5   The Duality Of Man 111
    5.1 The Human Being and the Spiritual Being 111
    5.2 The concept of the Holy Trinity............. 115
    5.3 The danger of falling into Temptation .. 116
    5.4 The Message of Love for the first time is given to the world 117
    5.5 The teachings of Jesus Christ are adulterated by the Church 122
    5.6 The revelation of God's name.................124
    5.7 Who am I? 125
Chapter 6   Meditation 131
    6.1 The Concept of Prayer 131
    6.2 The Art of Meditation 135
    6.3 Contemplative Meditation 137
    6.4 History of Meditation 141
    6.5 When can I realize God within me? 143

INTRODUCTION TO THE SECOND EDITION

The title of this book may seem presumptuous or, perhaps, an advertising strategy, but it's nothing like that. It is the secret of this human life that we are all living, a life full of ups and downs, joys and sorrows, triumphs and failures, health and disease, births and deaths. Daily, the media shows us cruelty without limits that exists between human beings, as well as the relentlessness of natural disasters (earthquakes, hurricanes, floods, pandemics, and others) that indiscriminately destroys entire families and that humanity has suffered for thousands of years. So, one may wonder where is the Almighty and Omnipresent "God" that different religions of the world present to us if one, as a human parent, would give anything for their loved ones to avoid suffering. The correct answer to that question will not be given by any religion. You will only find the Truth by studying the mystics of the world.

This book is based on the extraordinary revelations that mystics have left us throughout time. Mystics do not philosophize about God but *experience* God. They go to meet God in the depths of their being, in their consciousness, until they manage to merge with Him without losing their individuality. Achieving that unity with God is their only goal. Mystics are above religious dogmas. Despite the fact that some belonged to a different religion in the past, once their enlightenment was reached, they were separated or voluntarily separated from the religious community from which they originally came from.

The maximum exponents of mysticism are Gautama the Buddha of India and Jesus Christ, the Son of God, the Light of the world, who appeared in Judea some five hundred and fifty years later. Both reached a complete union with God.

In India, it has always been accepted that anyone can become Buddha (meaning the Enlightened One) or at least attain some measure of enlightenment. However, Gautama's teachings have been misinterpreted by his followers, who did not reach the level of spiritual awareness necessary to understand his teachings, so today, Buddhism and Hinduism do not fully reflect what Gautama taught.

On the other hand, when the Christian Church was organized around Jesus as a central figure, it was established that God incarnated only in Jesus, thus distorting the original message of Jesus and, consequently, keeping the Western world in spiritual darkness.

The world's religions have gone from being polytheists to monotheists. They went from asking their wishes to various gods and goddesses (as in Greek mythology) to asking only one God, but always preaching a dualism based on the battle between the right and wrong. Similarly, the same pagan rituals and practices are preserved for the purpose of trying to persuade a *rewarding-punishing god mounted up there in heaven, who does not exist*. It is incredible that there are still educated and intelligent people who continue to believe in that god of lies. The ignorance of the contemporary human being in spiritual matters is pathetic. This confirms to us that the *mind* cannot be used to find God. It is only the faculty of *spiritual discernment* that leads us to the encounter with God.

It happens to the human being as in the fable of Mount Olympus, which I mention in the first chapter of this book, that he cannot find divinity within himself. And he cannot find it because he is convinced that he is a creature separate and distinct from God, and this mistaken concept is what leads him to search for a lying god, a Superman, created by the fantasy mind of the human being. Consequently, the human being does not have the ability to recognize (let alone choose) the true God. That is why Jesus says to us in the name of God: **"You did not choose me, but I chose you"** (John 15:16).

The legacy of spiritual wisdom that mystics have revealed to us is something so extraordinary, so profound and so different from what we have been receiving for thousands of years from the different religions of the world, that it is extremely difficult to remove from human consciousness so many misconceptions, embedded in the collective subconscious. These misconceptions have been the cause of all the problems and misfortunes that we humans face in this material world on a daily basis.

The mystics discovered, within every man and woman, that there is a substance that is sacred: a light, a presence, a power, a spiritual consciousness, an invisible infinity, a God. The name is not important. The important thing is to know that all human beings have the potential to achieve an enlightened consciousness, as long as we have the determination to obtain it and put into daily practice the spiritual principles that mystics have written down to us both in the Bible and in the Bhagavad-Gita, the holy scripture of the Hindus. Nevertheless, despite all these extraordinary revelations of the spiritual principles and the Bible being the most sold and read book of all the times, humans are not yet in conditions to assimilate and put into practice such teachings. The prophecy of Isaiah is fulfilled, which says: **"Be ever hearing, but never understanding; be ever seeing, but never perceiving"** (Isaiah 6:9).

Jesus knew that his message could only be understood and practiced by a very small group of people. It is not a message for the masses. He tells us: **"These people honor me with their lips, but their heart is far from me. They worship me in vain; their teachings are merely human rules"** (Matthew 15:8-9).

As the crowds were in no condition to receive the Truth or reach an understanding, the Master Jesus spoke to them in the form of parables. When the disciples asked Jesus: "Why do you speak to them in parables?" referring to the crowds, Jesus responded by saying: **"Because the knowledge of the secrets of the kingdom of heaven has been given to you, but not to them. Whoever has will be given more, and they will have an abundance. Whoever does not have, even what they have will be taken from them. This is why I speak to them in parables: though seeing, they do not see; though hearing, they do not hear or understand"** (Matthew 13:11-13).

The human race's consciousness has been slowly evolving since prehistoric times when we lived in caverns. That primitive man evolved into a person more intellectually advanced until, at some point of his evolution, the inner light began to make its way into his material consciousness and put him on the spiritual path. Nevertheless, the human condition controlled by our mind is so strong that it has us convinced that this material world we live in exists outside of us. The truth is that everything we experience in our lives is in our consciousness. If we have a consciousness of Truth and Love, we experience God's activity in us; but if we accept the human condition of good and evil as real, that is what we will manifest in our experience in this life and in the next.

In the words of Joel S. Goldsmith, one of the most prominent mystics of the 20th century, **'Somewhere in consciousness there lies a land undiscovered, a land not yet revealed by religion, philosophy, or science. I know that it exists for it continually pushes itself into my awareness. I know that when it discloses itself, it will change the nature of mankind: wars will be no more, and the lamb will lie down with the lion. I know its name, for it is revealed as My kingdom or My grace. Christ Jesus spoke of this Kingdom, but neither the spoken word nor the manuscripts so far discovered have revealed its full significance "**(A Parenthesis in Eternity, p. 1).

Mystics make it clear to us that people have spiritual concerns, not because they deserve it, have earned it or are better than the rest of humanity, for that would be a sin of self-centeredness in the highest degree. God's finger has touched them for reasons that go far beyond their present experience on earth, reasons that have to do with the evolution of spiritual consciousness, which always manifests itself in each individual at their own time. No human effort will make us return to the Father's house; it is the Consciousness itself that takes us back.

There is a quote from the great prophet and mystic Isaiah that goes like this: **"From now on I will tell you of new things, of hidden things unknown to you"**(Isaiah 48:6). That quote precisely sums up the scope and purpose of this book. However, making you know intellectually new things and hidden things is only the beginning, but a very important step in a long road to the development of spiritual awareness. As you succeed in incorporating the principles described in this book into your consciousness, your consciousness will evolve into an increasingly enlightened consciousness. The only hope that we have to restore harmony in our lives is to return to a conscious union with God.

To those who this message does not touch their heart it is because their time has not yet come. People who have found interest in spiritual teachings have begun to question the validity of their desires or attachments to the things of this world. They have already experienced so many frustrations and dissatisfactions in their past human lives that they begin to question the meaning of human life and seek an answer that they cannot find in the religions. No one comes looking for this spiritual message in a single life. *This message is so spiritually elevated that the person has had to have some preparation in his previous life to be interested in it.*

Mystics say that from the moment you open a book about spirituality or have your first contact with a illuminated person, your own illumination has begun and any spiritual advancement that you achieve in this life, no matter how small it is, will multiply once you make your transition. I hope that, for you, this book is the beginning of your return to the Father's house.

This second edition repeats the same spiritual principles of the first edition, since spiritual principles are universal and eternal; they do not change. What has changed in this second edition is that the chapters have been divided into sub-chapters, which have been rearranged and, some have been expanded to facilitate their reading and understanding.

Any other kind of book would be obsolete with the new knowledge that appears after a relatively short time and that knowledge will be of no use to you once you leave this world; not so with spiritual knowledge, which is the one that will serve you once you make the transition to continue advancing in your spiritual development.

It should be noted that spiritual development is entirely individual. It cannot be done in groups or as a couple, nor does it depend on any guru or spiritual master. We help each other on our spiritual path, but each one goes alone to the center of his own being. Being on the spiritual path is the great adventure.

INTRODUCTION TO THE FIRST EDITION

For more than forty years, I have been in a diligent search for Truth, which I could not find in the Catholic environment in which I grew up. I have been a student of all the movements and currents that I have found in my investigations, ranging from spiritualism, which is communication with the dead, to metaphysics, through the Rosicrucian and Freemasonry. None of that satisfied me until I began studying the Bible and the mystics, who are those who communicate directly with God and who spiritually discern the hidden messages of the Bible, revealing to us their true meanings.

I am a student of mystics of all times, of all places and of all races, but I am far from being a mystic; I'm just trying, like you, to find my true spiritual identity. However, I have put into practice some of the spiritual treasures that mystics have revealed to us, with truly amazing results. In churches in San Jose, California, I have given testimonies of spiritual healings that I have had and lessons of humility that I have also received. What I am communicating to you here is a consequence of my experience in this field, small, but experience after all, not theory.

Several passages in the Bible alert us to false doctrines and prophets. Today, that need for alertness is even more valid, since, through the abundance of the media, we are overwhelmed daily with information of all kinds, including that misnamed "spiritual." Jesus, in Matthew 7:16, tells us how to protect ourselves from that: **"By their fruit you will recognize them."**

The benefits I have received from putting into practice some of the spiritual principles expressed in this book are those that give me the assurance that I am not guiding you wrongly; furthermore, what drives me to share these principles with you is the certainty that you will benefit enormously from them.

What I present to you here in plain language, without the pretensions of a writer, but directly and without disguise, are the most advanced spiritual principles that exist today. Some will be amazed at how revolutionary they may seem, just as people from six centuries ago would have been surprised if we had told them that the earth is round and revolves around the sun, something incomprehensible to the level of consciousness realized at that time.

My job is to give a didactic structure to the spiritual principles revealed by the mystics of the world, in order to facilitate the teaching and understanding of *the letter of Truth*, which is the first step to get to *know the Truth*, which it is what will set you free.

It is said in metaphysics that *"when the student is ready, the teacher will appear."* In the spiritual realm, there is a hierarchy in which there will always be apprentices taught by scholars, who, in turn, are taught by masters. In this way, the torch of Truth is passed from one to the other in an eternal and continuous chain. I humbly hope to be that scholar who helps you in the most important activity of your life, which is your spiritual development.

CHAPTER 1

The Spiritual Sense

1.1 JOURNEY TO OUR INNER WORLD

I want to invite you to undertake the most extraordinary, interesting, and transcendental journey that one can make in this life; *the journey towards our inner world since that is the only way to get to know God. There is no other way.*

Thousands of years ago, in ancient Egypt, the great teacher Hermes Trismegistus (contemporary of Abraham) proclaimed a fundamental truth about the universe: **"As above, so below; as below it is above to achieve the miracle of one thing."** That maxim, which is part of his well-known Emerald Tablet, implies that both heaven and earth, spirit and matter, the invisible and the visible form an intimately connected unit.

The apostle Paul in Hebrews 11:3 tells us that, **"What is seen was not made out of what was visible."** Meaning that all the things that you see when you look around this human world have their cause or origin in the *invisible*. For example, if you want to build a house, a car, a plane or anything material, first, you have to have it in your consciousness which is *invisible,* then you can make it visible through your mind. Otherwise you could not do it. Therefore, if you want to change something in the material world, you have to go to the cause that is *invisible*.

I invite you to begin the exploration of that *real but invisible world*, that is within each of us and from which we can never separate because it is an integral part of our own being. However, it cannot be detected by our five senses or our mind, but only by our *spiritual sense or spiritual consciousness*.

1.2 THREE LEVELS OF CONSCIOUSNESS

The human being operates on three different levels of consciousness: physical, mental, and spiritual. It's a continuum. The body is subject to mind control, and the mind and body are subject to spiritual control. This is a *spiritual law* which means it is a *universal law*, to which we are all subject to, and if we are not operating in this way then we are in violation of the universal law, of the divine purpose, and therefore we suffer the consequences of our *spiritual ignorance* that is manifested through the miseries and discord of our human life.

For example, people addicted to nicotine, alcohol, or drugs, their body is the factor that dominates the mind and spirit. When the body feels the need, it simply orders the mind to provide the drug, and the person manages to get it. Even though, technically, desire originates from the mind, once the body has experienced it, it will put its own demands on the mind. That is why we should not give our body addictive substances because that implies putting our body in command of our lives. In Romans 8:6, we read: **"The mind governed by the flesh is death, but the mind governed by the Spirit is life and peace."**

That is why the Alcoholics Anonymous program, for example, is based on the development of a *spiritual awareness* as the only way to combat addiction. In other words, a *spiritual awakening* is sought in the person as a requirement for that person to permanently change their behavior or way of acting. If there is no change in consciousness, there will be no change in the person's behavior.

Without a change in consciousness, there is no love for the family, fear of punishment, or rehabilitation courses that prevent that person from falling back into the temptation that has created so much suffering for them and their loved ones. Only the presence of God in your life can make the desired change.

Personally, I can tell you that I had never felt God so close to me before I went to an Alcoholics Anonymous meeting and listened to the testimonies of some of its members. Even in churches, I had not felt so close to God.

Without a change in consciousness, the human being will continue to enjoy the material things of "this world" and try to get more money, health, sex, power and fun. Jesus warns us in Matthew 7:13: **"For wide is the gate and broad is the road that leads to destruction, and many enter through it."**

This affirmation of Jesus is more valid today than ever because our modern world is full of distractions that occupy all our attention and time and do not leave us space for the contemplation of our inner world. It is only when the desire to know God has been awakened in the human being that one begins to feel content with oneself and does not feel the need of the material world.

1.3 HOW TO GET TO KNOW GOD

We have five physical senses: sight, hearing, taste, touch, and smell; they are our means of physical correspondence with the third-dimensional world around us. God gave us an additional instrument: our *mind*, which is the means, or tool, of intellectual knowledge that also serves to communicate with the outside world.

For the human being in general, educated or not, what really exists is what he can see, hear, taste, touch or smell, or what he can reason through his mind. Human beings are born prisoners of the mind and the five senses and never in life do we escape from these limitations.

In antiquity, the horizon was so real that it represented the edge of the world and no one risked straying from their immediate environment. Great thinkers of that historical period, such as Socrates (470-399 B.C.) and other pre-Socratic philosophers, thought that the earth was flat. If they had known that the earth is round and the laws of gravity and navigation, the man or the woman would have ventured long before Christopher Columbus to sail around the world and find unlimited wealth. However, due to their ignorance the human being remained for thousands of years confined within the limits established by their senses and mind.

Furthermore, those physical and mental faculties that God has given us can only be used for specific functions. For example, we cannot read a book with our ears, nor can we dig a ditch in the ground with our minds, and it does not occur to anyone to do so; however, we try to use the mind to reach God even though it was never designed for that. Furthermore, the mind is a barrier to reaching God.

The human being is trying to reach God with the wrong tool, because he does not know that he has another faculty that God gave us: our *spiritual sense, soul sense, spiritual consciousness or Christ consciousness* (all are synonyms), which in the English language is known as *spiritual awareness*. It is also known as the *seventh sense*. That is the sense that every human being needs to develop to get to know God, since God is spirit and can only be spiritually discerned; that is, it can only be grasped through our *spiritual sense*.

The apostle Paul tells us this clearly in I Corinthians 2:14: **"But the natural man does not receive the things of the Spirit of God, for they are foolishness to him; nor can he know them, because they are spiritually discerned."** In other words, through the mind you can never get to know God. *Spiritual discernment* is the power to see what is not evident with the mind. It is exclusively a faculty of the soul, of the spirit, which is within you but needs to be gradually developed. That is precisely our goal and for that purpose I wrote this book.

And notice that I say to "know" God and not "believe" in God, which is just an act of faith without being certain of his existence. Most people believe in God, but very few know God. "Knowledge" does not mean collecting intellectual information. "Knowledge" implies *experience*, hence the phrase: "*All knowledge is empirical*", that is, that *all knowledge comes from experience.*

In the words of Albert Einstein (1879-1955), *"Learning is experience, everything else is information."* We cannot know anything that we have not experience. You can memorize a manual of how to drive a car, but you will not know how to do it until you have the experience of driving. Similarly, to have knowledge of God we must have *the experience of God*. In other words, you will only "get to know God" when you have your own experience where God reveals himself to you from within your own consciousness.

1.4 THE FABLE OF MOUNT OLYMPUS

It is said that one day the gods on Mount Olympus were bored, and one of them proposed to create a toy that was like them. At first, they loved the idea, until one of the gods made the observation that if they made that toy in his image and likeness, then he was going to be divine and immortal too and someday he might be jealous of them and take away their Olympus. To this another of the gods replied that this problem could be avoided by hiding his divinity where he could never find it. The problem now was: where to hide his divinity?

"One solution," said one, "is to hide it on top of Mount Everest, where he can never find it."

"Don't forget," said another, "that he is going to be immortal and even though he won't be able to climb Mount Everest today, surely in three or four thousand years that immortal rascal will find a way to do it."

And so, several proposals were equally rejected for the same reason, until Juno told them:

--I know where to hide his divinity so that he can never find it: let's put it inside his own being.

And indeed they did.

Fortunately for us, seekers of divinity, there have been some men and women in the history of humanity who have been curious about the divine and did not rest until they found it.

Today we find, both in the Eastern and Western world, sacred writings and writings of mystics who have experienced God within themselves throughout our history.

In the Vedas, a collection of Hindu scriptures dating from approximately 1500 B.C., we read: **"He is not a God outside, but He is within."**

At the same time, we read in the Bible: **"For the Lord your God, it is He who goes with you. He will not fail you, nor forsake you"** (Deuteronomy 31:6). God said to Moses, **"My Presence will go with you, and I will give you rest"** (Exodus 33:14), and the prophet Ezekiel tells us what he received from God: **"I will put my Spirit within you"** (Ezekiel 36:27). Asked by the Pharisees, when the kingdom of God should come, Jesus answered them: **"The kingdom of God is within you"** (Luke 17:21) and, for his part, Paul asks us: **"Do you not know that you are the temple of God, and that the Spirit of God dwells in you?"** (I Corinthians 3:16). In Psalm 82:6, we read: **"You are gods; you are all sons of the Most High."**

The incredible similarity between the mystics of the world when they try to put into words their experiences with God is interesting, even though there may be hundreds or thousands of years between them. In contrast, theology, which literally means *"treatise or reasoned discourse regarding God"*, is nothing more than a set of mental speculations. Theologians use the mind to try to reach God, and that is impossible. Their opinions, as well as those of the philosophers and scientists who deal with the same subject, are nothing more than speculation, and there are as many opinions as there are different thinking minds. *Words about God are of no value unless they are based on God's experience.* The apostle Paul tells us: **"For the kingdom of God is not in words, but in power"** (I Corinthians 4:20). When the theologian, the philosopher, or the scientist achieve *the experience of God*, then they become mystics.

1.5 OUR TRUE IDENTITY

Today, *the human being remains ignorant of his true spiritual identity*, despite the fact that we have been created in the image and likeness of God. **"Then God said: Let us make mankind in our image, in our likeness"** (Genesis 1:26).

The Master Jesus confirms this in Matthew 23: 9, by forcefully revealing to us our true identity: **"And call no man your father upon the earth, for one is your Father, which is in heaven."** This affirmation of Jesus Christ could not be more encouraging for our spirit. Not even in our wildest dreams could we imagine such an extraordinary kinship. This is considered one of the most extraordinary affirmations of Jesus in revealing to us one of the essential spiritual principles of mysticism:

the principle of unity. There is the one and only Creator who is Spirit and is Infinite. There is no other. Making real in your conscience the principle of *"do not call anyone a father on earth, because only one is your Father"* automatically makes each man, each woman, and each child your brothers, because we are all by divine ordination, children of the same Father.

On the other hand, internalizing that truth is a liberation for all those who have had negative experiences with their human parents. Unfortunately, there are fathers and mothers who do not deserve such qualifications. However, reject all resentment and be careful to judge your human parents, even when they obviously deserve it, and remember that everyone does the best they can at their own level of *realized consciousness.*

By God making us in His image and likeness, our true nature is spiritual and perfect. Jesus ratifies it when he demands from us in Matthew 5:48: **"Be perfect, therefore, as your Father which is in heaven is perfect."** What a command from the master Jesus! Religious priests and Christian pastors have no way to explain that request of Jesus, as it contradicts everything they believe and preach. No human being is perfect, but as he makes way for the enlightenment within him, his spirituality displaces his humanity until he merges with God. *That is the truth about you and all of us!*

On the other hand, Jesus Christ points out to us that **"God is Spirit"** (John 4:24) and **"that which is born of the Spirit is spirit"** (John 3:6). Consequently, we are spirit, created in the image and likeness of God. We are not mortal or human beings but spiritual beings. God has not been able to create a human being, because God is Spirit and what is born of the Spirit is spirit. However, the entire world has the belief, held by different religions, that we are separate human beings and different from God. In the same way, we were convinced for thousands of years that the earth was flat. *In essence, humanity's fundamental problem is not knowing who we are.*

The Jesuit and mystic Pierre Teilhard de Chardin tells us: **"We are not human beings who have a spiritual experience. We are spiritual beings who are having a human experience."**

We need to awaken to our true spiritual identity. *The realization in our conscience of that Truth*, that is, making it yours beyond your mind, in your conscience, is of fundamental importance for your spiritual development and for your well-being. We need to *realize in our consciousness* (and not just know it intellectually) *that our humanity is just a disguise that covers our divinity*. The price that human beings are paying for our *spiritual ignorance*, shown in diseases, scarcity, insecurity, lack of love, frustrations, etc., is too high.

There is a Buddhist proverb that says: **"The cause of human suffering is ignorance. And the ignorance of oneself is the greatest of all ignorance."** And in words of William Shakespeare: **"There is no darkness but ignorance."** In fact, spiritual ignorance and superstition in religious matters are the most widespread teachings on earth, and it is what has kept us and continues to keep us apart from God.

1.6 THE PARABLE OF THE PRODIGAL SON

Our human experience is clearly represented in the parable of The Prodigal Son (Luke 15:11-32), which tells of the son who asks his father to give him his inheritance while he is alive and leaves the house to squander all his assets on things of "this world", until he is left with nothing. He spent all his human resources and, allegorically, ends up sleeping with the pigs, which for the Hebrews is the lowest that a person can go. The parable continues: **"And when he came to his senses, he said: How many of my father's hired servants have food to spare, and here I am starving to death!"** In other words, he had reached the extreme depths of his misery when he had a *spiritual awakening that made him realize his true identity.*

This is a wonderful lesson for all of us because it is an experience that all human beings go through. Sooner or later, we mortals will reach a point where we will feel God's need: **"As surely as I live, says the Lord, every knee will bow to me, and every tongue will acknowledge God"** (Romans 14:11).

The parable continues with the prodigal son saying: **"I will set out and go back to my father and say to him: Father, I have sinned against heaven and against you. I am no longer worthy to be called your son; make me like one of your hired servants. So he got up and went to**

his father." That homecoming symbolizes repentance, but it is actually more than that; it is a *change of consciousness*, which is what makes the son begin to walk in the direction of the Father's house.

The extraordinary thing about the story comes later: **"But while he was still a long way off, his father saw him and was filled with compassion for him; he ran to his son, threw his arms around him and kissed him."** This is the evidence of our Father's infinite and unconditional love for us, which does not make us pay to the last penny for our sinful actions, nor does it establish any condition in order to deserve his love. As prodigal children, we move away from our Father's house as much as we can, but when we decide to return, we do not have to retrace the entire distance traveled because "still being far away", our Father runs to meet us. The parable continues with the prodigal son saying, **"Father, I am no longer worthy to be called your son."** But the Father orders his servants to bring the best clothes and garments to dress him, and put on a banquet, **"For this my son of mine was dead and is alive again."** My son was dead!

1.7 HUMAN BEINGS ARE "WALKING DEAD"

For the mystics there are two kinds of people: the enlightened ones who are "alive" and live for eternity next to God, and the human beings who are the "walking dead," subject to their karma and the "wheel of life" which is the repeated cycle of birth and rebirth. Both our karma and the cycle of life end when we reach enlightenment or development of Spiritual Consciousness. Upon leaving the Father's house, the prodigal son became a walking dead. Unfortunately, the effect of his estrangement from his father is not immediately felt because he has inherited assets that allow him to lead a wasteful life until he runs out of material resources.

Similarly, in the allegory of the vine (John 15), the human being is compared to branches cut from the tree vine, which dry with time and are thrown into the fire. At the moment of being cut, there is still sap in the branches that continues feeding them for a specific time. The branches do not dry up immediately, nor does the prodigal son feel miserable immediately; there is always a time lapse between cause and effect. In a way, it is a disadvantage, because it makes us believe that we can live apart from God without any consequence.

When God created us, he gave us his substance, his inheritance, but the moment we acquired that *sense of separation*, we began to "dry up" and ended up in a very painful situation, since the cause of all our ills is *the perception of duality*. Not the duality itself, because that does not exist. However, by achieving that spiritual awakening in which Christ awakens in us, we begin to become alive and to know God. Jesus, in Matthew 22:32, tells us that **"God is not the God of the dead, but of the living"**, clearly indicating that human beings do not have God because in the eyes of God we only exist as spiritual beings. The apostle Paul demands of us: **"Wake up, sleeper, rise from the dead, and Christ will shine on you"** (Ephesians 5:14). And Psalm 17:15 tell us: **"When I awake, I will be satisfied with seeing your likeness."**

In that same order of ideas, we read in Matthew 8:21-22: **"Another disciple said to him: Lord, first let me go to bury my father"**, but Jesus told him, **"Follow me, and let the dead bury their own dead."**

Religious people who expect to live by the side of God when they leave this mortal world, will be in for a big surprise because they will continue to pay karma, life after life, as long as they continue in the opposite direction to the Father's House.

We, therefore, have only two paths to choose from: either we are moving away from our Father's house as "walking dead", separated and distinct from God by an act of our own conscience, which will inevitably end up sleeping with the pigs as in the parable of the prodigal son; or we are returning to our Father's house, also by an act of our own conscience, which we will inevitably reach if we stay on the spiritual path. It is only a matter of time and of our own dedication to the *study, meditation, and practice of spiritual principles*.

1.8 SPIRITUAL LIFE

Spiritual life is not achieved by quitting smoking or drinking or repeating the "Our Father" and "Hail Mary" many times, or attending church every Sunday or every day, or, as in the past, buying indulgences. If it were that easy, most people would have reached it by now. Jesus warns us when he tells us in Matthew 7:14: **"But small is the gate and narrow the road that leads to life, and only a few find it."** *Which leads to life!* Again, the concept of *walking dead* becomes evident.

Human beings think that they can add spiritual principles to their human consciousness (that is, to their way of being and thinking) and become spiritual beings, but that is not possible. Jesus clearly warns us in Matthew 9:17: **"Neither do people put new wine into old wineskins. If they do, the skins will burst; the wine will run out and the wineskins will be ruined. No, they put new wine into new wineskins, and both are preserved."** The new wineskins are a *new consciousness*. Jesus demands a change of conscience so that the seed of spirituality falls on fertile soil and is not lost.

Ancient concepts of God, such as that of an old man with a beard, sitting on a throne somewhere in heaven, who can be bribed by us to fulfill our wishes, and negative feelings such as hatred, resentment, envy, jealousy, malevolence, selfishness, prejudice, revenge, rancor, pedantry, arrogance, bigotry, fanaticism, fear, anxiety, etc., which are so ingrained in human consciousness, have to be uprooted to make way for that new consciousness essential for spiritual growth.

The apostle Paul tells us in I Corinthians 15:31 that the human being has to **"die daily"** to make way for the spiritual being. That is, *you have to empty your mind daily* of all those negative and egocentric thoughts where God has no entrance and let go of all anger, disgust, or resentment of the past through forgiveness. This is vital because it is the starting point with which we begin to prepare the ground to build up our *spiritual consciousness*, what is essential to get into "heaven."

There is a great truth taken out of the ancient wisdoms that is necessary to die in order to be reborn. Scholars of religions, who lack spiritual discernment to teach great spiritual truth, have been teaching a widespread religious belief that after the physical death of a person belonging to their congregation, the person is ready to go to "heaven" and live for eternity with God, as if eternity began from now on. It is these false interpretations that have kept, and still keep, humanity in spiritual darkness. The correct interpretation has nothing to do with the physical death of the body but rather the death of false concepts and beliefs of this human life. In other words, a *change of consciousness* is required because you cannot be the same human being today that you were yesterday and add God. That is not possible.

1.9 DEVELOPING A SPIRITUAL AWARENESS

Unfortunately, the *spiritual consciousness* is totally asleep in the human being. However, it can be developed through constant effort, personal dedication, and correct practice, just as we develop our minds and physical skills. Let us take the study of music or any other art as an example. Suppose you start piano studies and are given basic finger exercises, which you practice until you develop a particular skill. Later, you begin with the study of musical chords, adding the intellectual to the physical. Now you are already applying your mental and physical faculties to the study of music. Those who persevere in these studies for several years find that they have begun to develop something that goes beyond the mental and the physical, which is a *musical consciousness*. That musical consciousness has always been within the musician but in a latent state, and due to studies, dedication, and constant practice he has managed to awaken that faculty that was within himself.

Similarly, *mathematical consciousness* can be developed. You start by learning to add, subtract, multiply, and divide; then, after many years of advanced study and experience, you find that your mind has been raised to a higher level of mathematical consciousness, which goes beyond the existing barrier of intellectual information. Those breakthroughs in knowledge are what the Einsteins and Beethovens of the world produce.

However, of all our senses, *the spiritual sense* is the most difficult to develop. It is much easier to achieve anything in the material world than in the spiritual world. That should not surprise us, because since we were in the womb, our parents' first concern is for our physical and mental well-being. From the moment we are born, they begin to stimulate us physically and mentally to prepare ourselves to face this human world as best as possible and thus achieve a life equal to or better than theirs. From preschool to university, our preparation focuses on physical and mental development. What about the spiritual? Unfortunately, it is conspicuous by its absence. We confuse the spiritual with the religious and we make the mistake of sowing in the conscience of our sons and daughters the concept of a punishing-rewarding God separate and distinct from oneself, as well as other nonsense that comes to be an impediment to the spiritual development of our sons and daughters as they become adults.

1.10 THE CONCEPT OF PRE-EXISTENCE

It is impossible to achieve an artistic or scientific consciousness, much less a spiritual consciousness in a single human existence. I am not saying this to discourage you; rather, the mere fact that you are reading this book is a sign that in your past life, you planted a spiritual seed in your consciousness that is beginning to bear fruit.

The concept of pre-existence may seem strange to you, but it was perfectly acceptable in ancient times by the Hebrew people, as well as in the East. In Matthew 16:13-14, Mark 8:27-28, and Luke 9:18-19, Jesus asks his disciples, **"Whom do people say the Son of man is?"** (Jesus used that phrase from "The Son of man" in reference to the prophecy of Daniel 7:13-14 that refers to the Messiah as the son of man.) **"They replied: Some say John the Baptist, others Elijah, and still others Jeremiah or one of the prophets"** which clearly indicates that the idea of reincarnation was accepted in the Hebrew world.

In Matthew 17:10-13, the disciples ask Jesus, **"Why then do the teachers of the law say that Elijah must come first? Jesus replied: Elijah has already come, and they did not recognize him ... Then the disciples understood that he was talking to them about John the Baptist."**

In John 9:1-2, it reads: **"As Jesus passed by, he saw a man blind from birth. His disciples asked him: Rabbi, who sinned: this man or his parents, that he was born blind?"** Again the concept of pre-existence is present because a man who is born blind cannot be a sinner unless he has sinned in his past life.

One of the great myths of Judeo-Christian religious teachings is that the human being lives a single life. That is nothing more than a myth originally created to control parishioners through fear: "God gives you a single life so that you comply with all the regulations of our Church and if you don't you will be condemned to hell for eternity."

The truth is that what you are experiencing today is a small parenthesis in your eternal life, you have lived many lives in the past, and there will be many more of them in the future. You have lived before, and you will continue living later.

On the other hand, if you are going to live for eternity from now on as religions tell you, that also means that you have existed for eternity in the past because the eternal has no beginning or end. It can't be any other way. *You have always existed as an individual and will continue to exist as an individual for eternity.* You would be surprised to know the thousands of times you have had fathers and mothers, sons and daughters, husbands and wives, family and friends, wealth and poverty. So it should not surprise you when Jesus tells you in Matthew 23: 9: **"Call no man your father upon the earth, for one is your Father, which is in heaven."**

One of the legendary figures of World War II, General George S. Patton, said he remembered eight reincarnations as a warrior. In Patton's "Many Lives, Many Battles", he describes many battle events and places in great detail. His prowess and bravery on the battlefields made him the most feared and respected of the Allied Generals. One of the German generals wrote that General Patton had a sixth sense that often placed him far above German intelligence. Undoubtedly, he acquired that quality through his military experience of several previous lives. On one occasion, recalling the soldiers fallen in the war, he said: *"It is foolish and wrong to mourn the men who have died. Instead, we must thank God that such men live."* General Patton is proof that if you are convinced of your pre-existence, you automatically overcome the fear of death.

Jesus also tells us in John 8:58: **"Before Abraham was born, I am!"** indicating that the individual being coexisted with God forever. In mystical writings, it is said, *"Before God"*, meaning before man had any concept of God, *"I existed as an individual being"*. It should be noted that this individuality does not disappear as a consequence of our spiritual development, but, on the contrary, it enlarges as we give out to the infinite qualities of God. But those qualities should be understood as facets of God manifested through the person and not the personal qualities of the individual.

It is very important to distinguish between pre-existence and reincarnation. Reincarnation, as taught in some eastern schools, is regression, and that is a mistake. It is impossible to retreat from a *realized state of consciousness*, just as it is impossible for a rose to return to a bud. That is contrary to the laws of nature, that is, to the laws of God. Besides, God created us in His image and likeness to have dominion upon the earth, and created all animals and plants according to their species.

There are those who reject the concept of pre-existence because "we do not remember our past". However, neither do we remember our lives as babies, but that doesn't mean we didn't have a baby life. *We do not remember our previous lives because we have lived them wholly on the human plane.* Until we advance in our spiritual development, we will not remember periods of our previous spiritual life. According to the testimonies of the mystics, *the spiritual development that we reach in this life will serve as a foundation for greater spiritual development in the life that follows.* As we advance in our spiritual development, we begin to remember our past lives. Do not believe that people like Buddha, Jesus Christ, Isaiah, John, Paul, and other enlightened ones came into this world and reached their spiritual development in the course of a single life. It is impossible to achieve such a high degree of enlightenment without having established the necessary foundations in previous lives.

On the other hand, no other theory better explains the great divergence in the capacity to acquire knowledge that exists between human beings. We have said that knowledge is acquired only through experience, while our previous life experiences are recorded in our subconscious. We will speak of this extensively in subsequent chapters.

In looking at our human lives, we definitely have to take a long-term point of view. We cannot look at our life as a one-life event. At the human level, we are nothing more than the sum of our experiences acquired in previous lives, and from one life to another, we pay for our mistakes while also being compensated for our good works. Our previous life has had a direct impact on our current life, and so on. In the New Testament, this is known as the law of **"For whatsoever a man soweth, that shall he also reap"** (Galatians 6:7), in the Old Testament as **"Eye for an eye, tooth for tooth"** (Exodus 21:24) and in the East as the law of *karma*. In the next chapter, we will expand on this topic.

That "wheel of life", which Buddhists call *samsara*, is the repeated cycle of birth, life, death, and rebirth, with all the sufferings that it entails according to our karma or the quality of our actions and thoughts. It goes on and on until, tired of so much pain, like the prodigal son, we desperately search for a way out. *Always keep in mind that all the problems in our human lives have only one purpose: to offer us the opportunity to grow spiritually. There is no other reason.*

The exit or liberation from that cycle of transmigration of the spirit will only be achieved when we have reached enlightenment, or what the Buddhists call *nirvana* and the Japanese *satori*, which is the fusion of our soul with divinity. In other words, what definitively dissolves the bonds of karma in our lives is the development of *spiritual consciousness, Christ consciousness, Buddha-mind or satori*, or, what is the same, *experiencing the spirit of God within ourselves*. Without a doubt, it is the most difficult task ahead for us humans. There is no greater challenge in the world than that.

1.11 THE MOST IMPORTANT COMMANDMENT

The Pharisees attempted to trick Jesus when they asked: **"Master, which is the great commandment in the law?"** Jesus said unto them: **"Love the Lord your God with all your heart, and with all your soul, and with all your mind. This is the first and greatest commandment. And the second is like it: Love your neighbor as yourself. All the law and the prophets hang on these two commandments."** (Matthew 22: 37-40).

Actually, these *two commandments of Jesus* encompass the ten commandments of the Mosaic law and introduce the word *Love* to the world for the first time. Unlike the Old Testament that speaks to us of a punishing-rewarding God, Jesus introduces us to the God of Love. **"Your heavenly Father who makes his sun to rise on the evil and the good, and sends rain on the just and the unjust"** (Matthew 5: 45).

On the other hand, it is important to point out that Jesus is asked about a single commandment, the great of all the ten commandments. However, he does not give them one but two, and tells them that the second is similar to the first, that is, almost the same, since *loving one's neighbor is an indispensable condition for reaching God*. In this way, Jesus gives us the key to our spiritual development, by telling us that *we must love God and our neighbor*, because we cannot separate them from each other. *If you do not love your neighbor, you cannot love God.*

To love, in the mystical sense, is to experience, to realize the unity with God and with all His creation. Loving Him with all our hearts means pure, disinterested love, with no desire to get something in return. Loving him with all our minds means that there should be no more room in our minds than to contemplate and praise the Lord's work. **"Seek ye first the kingdom of God, and his righteousness; and all these things shall be added unto you"** (Matthew 6:33). If you can do this, you are in obedience to the spiritual law. This is extremely important, because human beings live in a *mental world*, as we will see in Chapter 4, "Man and his creation", and what we maintain in our *mental consciousness* is what manifests itself in our external world.

As for the second commandment, similar to the first, it should be clarified that *neighbor* refers to each human being, each animal and each plant on the earth, and even the earth itself. To the extent that you are loving your neighbor as yourself, to the same extent you are loving God and His creation, consequently, experiencing *unity* and not separation or duality, which is precisely the cause of the problems that we human beings are facing.

For example, consider a flower. Flowers do not exist independently floating in the air, rather, they exist only where there is a soil of a certain type, where there is water in a certain amount and where there is sunlight with a certain duration and intensity. All of these things form a unified field, a living system in constant movement and transformation. We can continue adding things to our example, let's say a bee. Bees do not exist if there are no flowers; and in turn contribute to the pollination of flowers. And so we can keep adding things until we have added all the things. That set: bee-flower-soil-water-earth-sun requires a galaxy for the sun and earth to exist, and the galaxy requires a universe. Thus the entire universe, every atom of animate and inanimate creation, forms an intimately connected unit. *There is no doubt that unity in variety is the plan of creation.*

Mystics have always maintained an attitude of reverence and respect for the nature around us, including for inanimate creation. Saint Francis of Assisi recognized his brothers and sisters in the sun, moon, stars, trees, and birds, and spoke to them with love. Saint Anthony of Padua preached to the fish and expressed his love for them. And from Sufism, Islamic mysticism, we have some beautiful verses that are a recognition and a praise to the omnipresence of God; they say: **"God** sleeps in the rock, / dreams in the plant, / stirs in the animal / and awakens in man"

1.12 LOVE YOUR NEIGHBOR

Each phrase of Jesus is a spiritual law or, the same, *a universal law* and must be taken very seriously because if we disobey it, we will infallibly pay for it. Each one of us must examine our own conscience and know if we are complying with the second commandment, similar to the first, to **"Love your neighbor as yourself."** This is of paramount importance because, regardless of nationality, religion, race, and color, we are all brothers. After all, we are children of the same Father. Jesus is emphatic about that when he asks us in Matthew 23: 9: **"Call no man your father upon the earth, for one is your Father, which is in heaven."**

It should be clarified that the *love* to which Jesus refers is not personal love, for an ethnic or religious group or a country. That is the human sense of love, which from the spiritual point of view is not love. *Divine love is unconditional, impersonal, and universal*, like the sun that lights all the gardens, not only yours and mine.

If you ponder in your mind that principle of *unconditional, impersonal and universal love* until you manage to register it in your consciousness, your conditioned human consciousness of prejudices would be cleansed, to the point that you would be universally *one* with your neighbor. *That truth would only be enough to transform your life and transform the planet.* If we look at each other as brothers and sisters, our life would be a life of love, service, devotion, and sharing. There is no greater force in the universe than *divine love*.

On the other hand, the concept of family that we human beings have, limited only to our first and second last names, has no place in the spiritual world. Moreover, this is another of the concepts that you have to remove from your consciousness to replace it with a much broader concept of family, which encompasses all creation.

When Jesus was told that his mother and brothers were outside and wanted to see him, he replied, pointing to the crowd: **"My mother** and my brothers are those who hear the God's word and put it into practice" (Luke 8:21). *And put it into practice!* In other words, it is not enough to listen to or read the word of God or spiritual principles, but you have to act on them; we have to force our minds to accept them, even if we still do not have the conviction of the truth of these principles.

Paul tells us in II Corinthians 3:6: **"Not of the letter, but of the Spirit: for the letter kills but the Spirit gives life."** That is to say, receiving only intellectually the Truth does not produce any spiritual fruit. You have to grasp the spirit of the letter and put it into practice to be able to reach the *experience of God*.

1.13 THE LAW OF FORGIVENESS

On the other hand, it should not be forgotten that the love for your neighbor is closely related to the law of forgiveness. A law, considered as one of the most significant laws revealed by Jesus Christ. Matthew 18:21-22 reads: **"Then Peter came to Jesus and asked: Lord, how many times shall I forgive my brother or sister who sins against me? Up to seven times? Jesus answered: I tell you, not seven times, but seventy times seven."** That is, always. We cannot be judging, condemning, and/or criticizing our neighbor because we immediately *experience separation*, distancing ourselves from God.

Let us not forget that our sins are forgiven insofar as we forgive those who sin against us. Jesus indicates this to us in Matthew 6:15: **"But if you do not forgive others their sins, your Father will not forgive your sins."**

It is necessary, then, to cease all kinds of resentment or hatred against people we consider our enemies, whether they are family, personal, racial, religious, political, national or international level. Instead, we are to make peace with them in our conscience. In Matthew 5:44-45, Jesus tells us: **"Love your enemies and pray for those who persecute you, that you may be children of your Father which is in heaven."** And later, he tells us that *loving those who love us has no merit*.

One wonders: which church, during World War I, World War II, and now against terrorism, has been or is praying for the enemy, fulfilling one of the most significant spiritual laws revealed to humanity? That does not mean that we are going to be defenseless victims of human beings who want to harm us in this world; there is no virtue in that. Virtue is in being able to see through the human being, including our enemies, the divinity of his spiritual being. That is, the Christ or the presence of God within each individual, regardless of external appearances, and make it real in our consciousness. That is sowing in the spirit and not in the flesh. *That is spiritual discernment.* In this way, we fulfill the second greatest commandment: **"Love your neighbor as yourself"** (Matthew 22:39). That allows us to rise spiritually to where evil cannot reach us.

1.14 SPIRITUAL POWER IS ABSOLUTE

"For the battle is the Lord's" (I Samuel 17:47); This is what young David said when, being just a teenage sheepherder, he faced (with an insignificant sling but full of a conviction from his *God-conscious realization*) the giant Goliath, who was almost three meters tall, heavily armed and protected with armor and helmet, and considered invincible among the armies. **"You come against me with sword and spear and javelin, but I come against you in the name of the Lord"** (I Samuel 17:45). What David was saying was: *"I do not come with weapons or physical power; I only come in the name of the Almighty."* That is the secret: to remain firm in the conscious realization of God's omnipresence in whose presence there is no other power.

In the Bible, we find numerous examples in which *spiritual power* defeats the forces of evil. A significant event was the invasion of Judah by Sennacherib, king of Assyria (701-693 BC), who seized all the fortified cities and besieged the city of Jerusalem with his powerful army (the largest at the time), urging Hezekiah, King of Judah, to surrender or to be annihilated. Next to Hezekiah, who was an enlightened king, was the prophet and mystic Isaiah (called the evangelist prophet by his many messianic predictions). He transmitted to Hezekiah the message he had received from God: **"I, the Lord, I declare that the king of Assyria will not enter this city, nor will he launch a single arrow against it"** (Isaiah 37:33); This encouraged Hezekiah to say to his people, **"Be strong and courageous, be not afraid nor dismayed** for the king of Assyria and his large army, for he who is with us is more powerful than he who is with him. With him is an arm of flesh, but with us is the Lord, our God to help us"(II Chronicles 32:7-8). And in the Bible, we are told: **"Hearing Hezekiah's words, the people trusted his words"**. In Isaiah 37:36 it reads: **"Then the angel of the Lord went out and killed one hundred and eighty-five thousand men from the Assyrian camp."** These events have been recorded not only in the Bible but also in Sennacherib's account of his invasion of Judah, exhibited in the museum of the Oriental Institute in Chicago. In that account, Sennacherib admits that he never captured the city of Jerusalem, even though he sent his great army against it; Biblical historians point out that a great plague forced the army to withdraw.

The intervention of angels, either directly or through different manifestations, is frequent in numerous passages of the Bible, both in the Old and New Testaments. When Jesus is sought by the bailiffs of the Jewish priests in the garden of Gethsemane who wanted to put in prison, and Peter tries to intervene to defend him, Jesus tells him: **"Put your sword back in its place, for all who draw the sword will die by the sword. Do you think I cannot call on my Father, and he will at once put at my disposal more than twelve legions of angels? But how then would the Scriptures be fulfilled that say it must happen in this way?"** (Matthew 26:52-54). Ironies of the human being! It was not enough for the Scriptures to be fulfilled to the letter and three years of miraculous healings throughout the Kingdom of Judah. More than two thousand years later, the Hebrews are still waiting for the Messiah.

1.15 THE SECRET OF YOUR SECURITY: "PRAY WITHOUT CEASING"

The development of a spiritual consciousness, even to a small degree, protects us from being victims of people or circumstances. But to achieve this, we have to remove from our human consciousness all the old concepts and negative feelings that block our communication with God.

When you leave your house in the morning to go to work, you are not sure that you will return at night. No matter what country or city you live in, anything can happen to you. Is there any way to avoid this? The Bible tells us that there is and tells us how to do it:

The Bible tells us that **"Whoever dwells in the shelter of the Most High will rest in the shadow of the Almighty"** (Psalm 91:1). This psalm does not promise immunity to all, but only to those who, day and night and day after day, live in the Word, and let the Word dwell in them. No one else has security in this world. But we must always be alert, attentive day by day and at every moment, so as not to accommodate or entertain negative thoughts or feelings that would immediately separate us from God.

In Isaiah 26:3, we are told: **"You will keep in perfect peace those whose mind is stayed on thee."**

And in Proverbs 3:6, we read: **"In all thy ways acknowledge Him, and He will direct thy paths."**

Spiritual power is an absolute power. There is no physical power or mental power that can be confronted. The Scriptures affirm it very clearly: **"If you say, 'The Lord is my refuge', and you made the Most High your dwelling, no harm will overtake you, no disaster will come near your tent. For he will command his angels concerning you to guard you in all your ways."** (Psalms 91:9-11).

These quotes from the Bible literally express the truth. God keeps us physically, mentally, morally, and financially at peace to the extent that our thoughts are focused on spiritual realities and not on the problems of material life. But that is not easy, because the human world that surrounds us overwhelms us daily with negative things that must be rejected immediately with a **"Away from me, Satan"**, following the example of Jesus in Matthew 4:10. Satan is understood not as the religious and childish concept of the rebellious angel who sabotages the creation of God, but the *temptation* to believe that we have a personal ego. We can just as well say, **"Away from me, temptation"**. That is the true devil, the product of *universal hypnotism*, which we will see in detail in Chapter 4 and of which we human beings are victims since it creates the illusion that we are separate and distinct beings from God. That has no power because the only power is God, but it does tempt us daily. For mystics, there is only one "I," and that "I" is God, not a person, man or woman. That "I" is the universal "I." There is a single "I," a single ego in the entire universe, a single life, a single power, and that is God. Jesus revealed a universal truth to us when he tells us in John 10:30: **"I and my Father are one."** There is no separation but only the illusion created by our mind and by our ego. We and the universe are ONE. One way to visualize this Truth is by imaging an immensely large Sun covering the entire infinite universe. The Sun says to the ray of light: ray of light you have light, you have heat and everything else that I have. My Life is your life, my Soul is your soul, my Being is your being, even my Body is your body. We are all ONE. All that I have is yours but you by yourself have nothing; not even your own existence. So is our relationship with God.

Once the person has imbued their mind in studying the word of Truth, the next step is to put those principles into practice in their daily life. **"Pray without ceasing"**, the apostle Paul tells us (I Thessalonians 5:17). *This means that we must always practice the presence of God in our conscience.* That does not mean that we will neglect our human duties or obligations and activities. *This means that we must maintain the omnipresence of God at all times, even when we are executing our daily tasks.*

For example, when we are in front of the steering wheel in our car, we must pause for a moment before starting the vehicle's engine to understand that it is God who is behind the wheel, through us and through all the drivers we are going to meet in our way, and maintain at all times the omnipresence of God. In this way, we protect ourselves from automobile accidents. **"A thousand may fall at your side, ten thousand at your right hand; but it will not come near you"** (Psalms 91:7).

When we look at the trees, flowers, mountains, and oceans, we train our minds to contemplate the Lord's work: **"The earth is the Lord's, and everything in it, the world, and all who live in it"** (Psalms 24:1). In contemplating the vastness of the sea, the mountains, the lakes, and the flowers, we manage to understand the psalmist's vision that the earth and everything in it belong to the Lord. This raises us in consciousness above the noises of this world and helps us feel God's presence.

Even if we have a bad boss at work, we try to look and address the Christ within him, that is, the presence of God within him. Every time you are in front of your boss or think about him, say to yourself: *"My Christ greets your Christ"*. You will soon notice a positive change in your life. In this way, we force our minds to contemplate the presence and activity of God in all things and in all the people around us, and we do not allow external appearances to disturb our peace and alter our state of consciousness, by diverting our attention towards the human world around us.

Furthermore, we read in the press or see on television every day the evil nature of some rulers in a position to manipulate the world; don't let that disturb you. Follow the example of Jesus when he was on the cross: **"Father, forgive them; for they do not know what they are doing"** (Luke 23:34). Reject appearances with a *"Get away from me, Satan"* and think about your true spiritual identity. Meditate for a while until you achieve your inner peace. The important thing is to eliminate any effect that those rulers may have on your conscience, as well as on the conscience of those who are in tune with yours. We can only be responsible for our state of consciousness. That is entirely our responsibility.

In this way, we keep dwelling on the Word, and there will not be a moment throughout the day that we do not consciously keep God alive in our minds. A constant reminder that *God is the omnipresent, omnipotent, and omniscient Spirit who created, maintains and sustains the real universe.* **"Abide in me, and I in you"** (John 15:4). When you realize in your conscience the universal "I" that is God, you will be able to travel to any part of the world, and you will always be in peace, harmony, and prosperity.

Hawaiian mysticism, known as Ho'oponopono, is a thousand-year-old practice that requires us to say all the time and to all people and to all things: **"I'm Sorry. Please forgive me. Thank you. I love you"**. You say that mentally to the divinity, that is everything. It is a way of fulfilling what the apostle Paul requires of us to **"pray without ceasing."** However, mentally repeating it like a mantra has no effect because it is a mental activity, but if you manage to do it in your consciousness, you will be surprised how your external world changes for the better.

Praying, according to the mystics, is not asking God to grant us something from this material world, since you are not going to infinite wisdom, which is all love, to indicate what you want for yourself or yours. Furthermore, that would be like insulting God, thinking that you have more compassion than Him. *You go to God in silence, with your mind empty, to listen to Him.* That is what is called *meditation*, and it is the most important practice in your spiritual development.

Through meditation, we will receive the truth from within ourselves, directly from the source: **"Speak, Lord, for your servant is listening"** (1 Samuel 3:9).

In this way, we go from knowing the truth intellectually, through the mind, to an inner awareness of the truth that comes from within ourselves. It is what the mystics call the "small and soft voice" and that Elijah mentions in I Kings 19:12 as **"A still small voice."** Those who have achieved that direct communication with God are the ones who have left us these spiritual treasures that allow us to start our journey in the right direction.

A very beloved, very Catholic sister (r.i.p.), already in years, told me one day that she did not mind dying because she was then going to "know God." I reminded her that God is omnipresent, that he is everywhere here and now, but that we must learn to see him with spiritual eyes. She did not answer me; she just fell silent. That is precisely the problem of religions that teach you a God separated and far from you, even with a human appearance, thus preventing your spiritual development.

In the Old Testament, we read: **"Yet in my flesh I will see God"** (Job 19:26). Here and now, at this very moment, we can see God. Of course, not with our physical eyes, but with our faculty of *spiritual discernment*. We can discern or be aware of its omnipresence. That is what it means to see or feel God, both in this life and in the next.

You have to be thirsty to know the truth, have the experience of God, and become "face to face" with God. **"And you shall know the truth, and the truth shall make you free"** (John 8:32). In that statement of Jesus, truth is synonymous with God. Now, knowing the truth is entirely your responsibility. The truth alone will not set you free; you have to be dedicated and make an intentional effort to experience it, and only then the truth will set you free. You will only know God when He has revealed Himself to you from within you. *Remember that God is an experience, not a concept or a belief.*

My purpose in writing this book is to introduce you to *the correct letter of truth*, which is what is known as *metaphysics*. This is the first essential step because it is to teach you the truth intellectually through your mind, revealing to you the existence of spiritual principles that are eternal and immutable. We try to satisfy the mind by answering all its questions through the correct interpretation of the Scriptures according to the mystics of the world. However, *intellectually knowing these spiritual principles is not enough.*

To benefit from these eternal and immutable spiritual principles, you have to start putting them into practice in your daily life, and it will be your dedication, your perseverance and your daily meditation on these spiritual principles that will help you realize the truth in your conscience, which is what will set you free. In this way, the prophecy of Isaiah 54:13 is fulfilled: **"All your children will be taught by the Lord and great will be their peace."** That is what is known as *mysticism*.

CHAPTER 2

God

2.1 FALSE CONCEPTS ABOUT GOD

It is incredible the diversity of wrong opinions and concepts about God that we continuously hear through the media and even within our circle of friends and family. The Christian religions describe an implacable "God", ready to condemn us to live for eternity in hell if we do not comply with the norms or precepts of its different denominations. *"Outside the Church, there is no salvation"* is a fundamental dogma or principle of Catholicism, as well as the Protestant Churches. This expression comes from Saint Cyprian of Carthage, theologian, bishop of the 3rd century and father of the Church. If that were not enough, they offer you only one chance in this life: either you accept their "God", with all the human regulations that have been invented, or you will be *condemned to eternal death in hell*. For anyone with a minimal sense of justice, that is a true monstrosity. Undoubtedly, the spirit of the Holy Inquisition is still present today among religious fanatics.

According to the Center for the Study of Global Christianity, in 2000, there were 34,000 Christian denominations, which are considered divisions within Protestant Christianity, and in 2017 they had increased by 32%. Even though they profess the same Christian faith, these denominations present rivalries between them, to the point of affirming that their precepts are the only ones that lead to salvation.

This proliferation of denominations can be explained, on one hand, by the fear of the unknown that is universal, which leads most people to seek protection in religions, and, on the other hand, because it is a very lucrative business. Most of these denomination's leaders do not require any special education, enjoy tax privileges, and practice the free interpretation of Scripture, manipulating the masses with a fear of everlasting punishment to collect tithe to "sustain the work of God," as if God required human help.

In a recent investigation, carried out by Univision and broadcast on television on December 2, 2018, under the name "Los Magnates de Dios", millionaire evangelical pastors were denounced. They own planes and mansions in Colombia, Guatemala, Nicaragua, El Salvador, Mexico, and the United States, and have been exploiting the spiritual ignorance of millions of low-income Hispanics who donate 10% of their monthly income to save their souls. These humble, uneducated people act without thought, with no free will, uniting their conscience to a hypnotized collective conscience under the persuasive and mental power of an unscrupulous leader. It is a typical case of mass psychology, where the individual ceases to be independent and subordinates themselves to the group to which they belong. In the words of one of those pastors' collaborators, "We don't need smart people here who question anything. We need brutes that don't question anything; everything is by mystery, and everything is by faith."

On the other hand, we have the argument of the atheist, which is much stronger and healthier than that of the religious fanatic who terrifies weak minds. The atheist denies God's existence because when they look around, they see are natural disasters, diseases, wars, terrorism, tyrannies, murders, rapes, children who are born deformed or blind, and others who are starving, etc. And so they ask themselves: where is God? It is a very valid question: when judging by appearances, the atheist judges very well; however, the conclusion they reach is wrong.

Human beings mistakenly believe that the concept we have of God in our minds is the true God. That mental concept that we have of God can be the image of a God-man with a white beard sitting on a cloud or a man with long hair that we identify as Jesus Christ or other concepts that the different world religions have been propagating for centuries. Those are misconceptions, and the worst thing is that we pray to those images in our minds in hopes of receiving an answer. Is that reasonable?

The Old Testament is full of stories of people and nations, asking God to destroy their enemies. As long as people believe that there is a Jewish God, a Catholic God, a Muslim God, or any other religion, we will be surrounded by bigotry and fanatism. *There is only one God. And God is not influenced by man, nor does he take orders from man, whatever his religion or race.*

The hierarchs of the Jewish religion reacted violently when they heard Jesus preach that God does not like animal sacrifices or monetary donations. Back then, people thought that God had to be pleased and appeased. They believed that God could be influenced in some way by their behavior to get Him to act on their behalf by granting their requests.

The modern man still asks God in the same way that our pagan ancestors did thousands of years ago. Religious devotees light candles, pay the tithe, observe days of abstinence, and impose all kinds of penances, thinking, perhaps subconsciously, that they can influence God for their benefit. Even today, most people try to use God, if not to destroy their enemies, to cure diseases, solve economic, sentimental, or any other problems. But God is not a person with human feelings who is waiting for our pleas to intervene. *That God does not exist.*

All the religions of the world teach a God who punishes the bad and rewards the good. *That God does not exist either.* God does not reward virtue or punish sin. **"For God, is no respecter of persons"** (Acts 10:34). God is God of the saint and of the sinner, of the just and of the unjust. The teacher Jesus says it clearly: **"Your heavenly Father who makes his sun to rise on the evil and on the good, and sendeth rain on the just and on the unjust"** (Matthew 5:45).

Never fear approaching God because you have sinned or are sinning; on the contrary, seek his presence to give you strength and not let you fall into temptation. Do not believe for a moment that God would turn away from you for your past or present sins. It is important that you understand the concept that God neither rewards you nor punishes you because it is an essential step in your spiritual development.

2.2 KARMA OR LAW OF CAUSE AND EFFECT

The truth is that sin is punished by sin itself, not by God. In other words, the person who makes the wrong electrical connection and gets burned cannot blame electricity. The person who goes into the sea without knowing how to swim and almost drowns cannot blame the sea. In both cases, it is the ignorance of these people that endangers their lives. In the same way, no one can violate spiritual laws and not be punished for such violations. *Guilt and punishment fall on the ignorant behavior of the individual, but God does not intervene.* What's more, God doesn't even know it.

One of the first laws to be learned in this spiritual quest is that on the human level there is what is known in the East as *karma* (karma in Sanskrit means "action") and in philosophy as *the law of cause and effect*. In the Old Testament, this law is referred to in Exodus 21:24 as **"An eye for an eye and a tooth for a tooth"** and in Ecclesiastes 11: 1 it is said: **"Cast thy bread upon the waters, for you shalt find it after many days."** In the New Testament, Jesus at no time mentions a punishing God but tells us in Matthew 7:2: **"For with what judgment ye judge, ye shall be judged; and with what measure ye mete, it shall be measured to you again"**, but not by God but by the law that establishes that **"for whatsoever a man soweth, that shall he also reap"** (Galatians 6:7). This law of cause and effect, for being a law at the human level, also has its equivalent in physics with Newton's third law, which says *that all action has an equal and opposite force of reaction.*

The God mentioned in the Old Testament is not God but the *karma or law of cause and effect*, which eventually makes us pay for the bad things we have done and rewards us for the good things we do. It is not God, rather our own level of consciousness, which encloses our most intimate thoughts and actions, which sets in motion the law of cause and effect of good and evil. The level of consciousness that we express whether through actions or thoughts, both in this life and in our previous lives, constitutes what is called our *karmic bank*, which sooner or later returns to ourselves. The bread that we throw in the waters is the bread that comes back to us. That law applies not only to individuals but also to nations, and even to the entire human race.

The story of Noah's ark is an example of the law of cause and effect in action. It is not the story of a God who saved an individual and his family and destroyed the rest of the world. When most people in a city or nation live contrary to the love of thy neighbor, any tragedy, natural or not, can eventually be expected to remove the evil from them. Another example from the Bible is the destruction of Sodom and Gomorrah. More recently, we have Nazi Germany and the evil empire of the Soviet Union. But don't hold God responsible for those actions, because God is too pure to have favorites.

Now that we are aware that there is a law of cause and effect or karma, to which all human beings are subject, our first task should be to harmonize with it. We must not forget that the universe is the echo of our actions and our thoughts. If you act with good, you will receive good; If you act with evil, sooner or later, you will receive evil. Consequently, if there is a punishment for stealing, we should not steal; If there is a punishment for lying, we should not lie, even if we get some temporary benefit because sooner or later, we will pay for it. That is nothing other than living on the level of a moral conscience that Moses established for the Hebrew people in order for them to recognize the difference between good and evil and act in accordance with good. The Ten Commandments that Moses received from God on Mount Sinai, and that he presented to his people three months after their departure from Egypt are:

"Thou shalt have no other gods before me"; "Thou shalt not make unto thee any graven image"; "Thou shalt not take the name of the Lord thy God in vain"; "Remember the Sabbath day, to keep it holy"; "Honour thy father and thy mother"; "Thou shalt not kill"; "Thou shalt not commit adultery", "Thou shalt not steal", "Thou shalt not bear false witness against thy neighbor", "Thou shalt not covet thy neighbour's house or thy neighbour's wife" (Exodus 20).

The first four commandments refer to our relationship with God, while the following six commandments refer to our relationship with our neighbor. Being obedient to the Ten Commandments brings us in harmony with the law of cause and effect, and we benefit from it. However, any violation of those Commandments tomorrow will bring us trouble. In his famous Sermon on the Mount, Jesus warns us: **"Think not that I am come to destroy the law, or the prophets; I am not come to destroy but to fulfill. For verily I say unto you, Till** heaven and earth pass, one jot or one tittle shall in no wise pass from the law, till all be fulfilled "(Matthew 5: 17-18)

2.3 THOUGHTS ARE ACTIONS

Every thought or action we take sets in motion the law of cause and effect or karma. Furthermore, each thought, feeling, and word contains an enormous vibratory force capable of affecting the body and the affairs of the human being.

Thoughts have consequences! Never forget that. I want to emphasize that thoughts, desires, and/or feelings are actions. The Master Jesus, continuing with the Sermon on the Mount, tells us in Matthew 5:21: **"You have heard that it was said to the people long ago, 'You shall not murder', and anyone who murders will be subject to judgment. But I tell you, that anyone who is angry with a brother or sister will be subject to judgment."** And in Matthew 5:27, he tells us: **"You have heard that it was said, 'You shalt not commit adultery.' But I tell you that anyone who looks at a woman to lustfully has already committed adultery with her in his heart."**

The apostle Paul, who received from Jesus the mission to evangelize the Gentiles, summarizes the law of cause and effect or karma in the following way:

- **"Whoever sows to please their flesh, from the flesh will reap corruption"** (Galatians 6:8). It means that putting faith and trust in family, friends, political influences, or any form of human dependency is sowing to the flesh and that we will reap corruption because someone will betray or fail us when we least expect it. In the Scriptures, we read: **"When my father and my mother forsake me, then the Lord will take me up"** (Psalms 27:10). In the human world, it is possible to find parents who abandon their children and children who abandon their parents. Never hope to gain any benefit from any human being, **"Cease ye from man, whose breath is in his nostrils"** (Isaiah 2:22). Similarly, if we place our hopes on man-made things, such as crucifixes or stars or any other symbol of religious belief, sooner or later, we will be disappointed. It is these disappointments and frustrations that abound in the human being. So putting our thoughts in any external way activates the law of cause and effect of good and evil that will lead us to discord and disharmony because we are sowing in the flesh.

- **"Whoever sows to please the Spirit, from the Spirit will reap eternal life"** (Galatians 6:8). You sow to the Spirit when you come to recognize that the soul of man is God. Our thoughts, our hopes must always be in God. That does not mean becoming ascetic and leaving our job, profession, home, or family. It has nothing to do with what we do externally, but with what is happening in our consciousness when our minds and bodies are performing their tasks on the external plane. What we have in our conscience is what determines whether we are sowing to the flesh or sowing to the Spirit. *Your life is your externalized consciousness.* Your life will never change until your consciousness changes.

We don't always reap what we sow immediately. It is said that *"the mills of the gods grind slowly; however, the grinding is extremely fine."* It is true that sometimes a person can walk for many years on the spiritual path without seeing the expected results, but that should not discourage us, because we must not forget that we have many previous human lives that must be cleaned from our conscience. On the other hand, there may be people doing evil for a long time before the law of cause and effect begins to operate; besides, we do not know what is in their bodies, their minds, or their souls. It can be much worse than we think. In any case, *the law of cause and effect adjusts all these things in its own time and in its own way.*

In other words, *we create our future today*. The law of cause and effect that we set in motion with our actions and/or thoughts will return to us tomorrow, next year, or next century, but surely there will be no escape if we violate the Ten Commandments or the Spiritual laws. *We must not forget that in sin is penance. Karma never forgets!*

To answer the question of how much do I have to pay for all my previous sins of omission or commission. The answer is encouraging: **"Though your sins are like scarlet, they shall be as white as snow"** (Isaiah 1:18). When? *Now, at the very moment of our repentance.* The thief on the cross was not condemned to a period of purgatory or any suffering: **"Today you will be with me in paradise"** (Luke 23:43). The woman accused of adultery became a follower of Jesus Christ at the moment of her repentance, without any waiting period and without any punishment. It should be noted that at that time in the Hebrew religion, only two sins were punishable by death: murder and adultery (of women). However, Jesus, ignoring the law and the pressure of Scribes as well as the Pharisees who had brought the adulterous woman to condemn her, said to them, **"Let any one of you who is without sin be the first to throw a stone at her"** (John 8:7). Hearing this, they withdrew one after another. Then, Jesus said to the woman: **"Neither do I condemn you; go, and sin no more"** (John 8:11), but with the warning *"sin no more,"* because something worse can happen to us.

In the Oriental teachings, the karma that you sow, especially the bad karma, remains with you for many, many lifetimes, until who knows what it takes to finally to erase it. That is not true. Jesus Christ revealed and showed us that all your bad karma, all your former wrong thinking or wrongdoing is wiped out in a moment of *repentance.*

Now, *repentance* does not only mean grieving, or being sorry or sad for what you have done and asking forgiveness from the aggrieved. Repentance means that and much more; it means that you have had *a change in the level of consciousness*, and from that very moment, you have taken a different and definitive turn in your life. Remember the parable of the prodigal son.

It should be clear to us that God has nothing to do with the law of cause and effect or karma. God neither punishes nor rewards. However, Protestants and Catholics still accept the old concept of the Hebraic God of the Ten Commandments or the punishing-rewarding God.

How many times have we heard that the accidental death of a person or the premature death of a baby is the "will of God!" Such a concept reflects, at best, great ignorance of the nature of God, and, at worst, a blasphemy. First of all, God is not aware of our sins or our illnesses. For the Father, the prodigal son never left his home. *Sin is punished for sin itself, and we are punished because in our spiritual ignorance we break spiritual laws.*

2.4 GOD IS

When we say that God is love, is life, is health, is our father, as Jesus calls Him, or mother Kali, as the great Hindu mystic Ramakrishna calls Him, we are not defining God or assigning masculine or feminine gender. Still, we are merely describing facets or attributes of God. Precisely because it is *the infinite nature of God*, it encompasses all these things and much more. The Hebrew philosopher and theologian Maimonides (1135-1204) say that when we try to describe God with all these attributes, we are only saying *"God is."* The great Chinese mystic Lao-Tse (604-521 BC) tells us: *"If you can define it, it is not God."* Some mystics refer to God as *the invisible infinity*; in this way, we avoid forming images in the mind. No image that can be conceived in the mind can be God. Actually, as another mystic says, God is a three-letter word that is useful because it means nothing; it must be *"without-concept."*

The human mind, being finite, is incapable of grasping the infinity of God, and that is what makes the human being by nature idolatrous. All the religions of the world have a personal God, and next to that, God comes with the idea of worship and devotion. The reason is that the human being tries to understand the abstract through thought-form or symbols. All external manifestations of religions, such as bells, music, rituals, books, images, etc., are part of that category of symbols. So, anything that is attractive to man's senses, anything that helps the human being to form a concrete image of the abstract is taken and worshiped. That is why, even though there have been reformers in all religions who have preached, from time to time, against symbols and rituals, their preaching has not been heard.

However, these symbols could initially help people who are beginning to develop their *spiritual sense or spiritual faculty or seventh sense* (they are all synonyms). Among the mystics, it is accepted that you were born in a church but not that you died in it, because that shows that you have not grown spiritually or, what is the same, that there has not been a development of your soul and you have lost your reincarnation.

I must clarify that my intention with this book is not to depart from or to renounce any church that, in your current level of consciousness, you are enjoying in association with people who share with you a particular religious belief. My purpose is to teach you *the letter of Truth*, revealed by Jesus Christ and other mystics of the world, and how to reach that Truth. **"You shall know the Truth, and the Truth shall make you free"** (John 8:32).

2.5 WHAT IS THE BEST RELIGION?

The Brazilian theologian and former Franciscan priest Leonardo Boff, who is one of the renovators of Liberation Theology, that encourages the Catholic Church to become politically and economically involved for the dispossessed, tells us that in the interval of a round table on *"Religion and Peace among the peoples"*, he asked with some malice but also with theological interest to the Dalai Lama: *"Your Holiness, what is the best religion?"* He expected him to answer Tibetan Buddhism or other Eastern religions much older than Christianity but was surprised when he replied: *"The best religion is the one that brings you closer to God, to infinity. It is the one that makes you better."*

Boff himself tells that, to get out of puzzlement at such a wise answer, he asked him: *"And what is it that makes me better?"* The Dalai Lama replied: *"What makes you more compassionate, more sensitive, more detached, more loving, more humanitarian, more responsible, more ethical. The religion that gets that from you is the best religion."*

In other words, being a good person and a good citizen who fulfills their duties and obligations that they have towards others also comply with Jesus' second commandment to *"love your neighbor as yourself"*, which is a condition sine qua non, inescapable to reach God. If you do not have love for your neighbor in your heart, you are very far from reaching God. Jesus Christ himself told the Hebrews that being a good Jew attached to his religious doctrine is not enough: **"For I say unto you, that except your righteousness shall exceed the righteousness of the scribes and Pharisees, you shall in no case enter into the kingdom of heaven."** (Matthew 5:20).

The scribes and Pharisees were perhaps the most religious people of their time. How could anyone exceed their religiosity when they were distinguished by their severity in the interpretation and practice of the Mosaic law. They were the best Hebrews in the synagogue, as they lived their entire lives in the temple, obeying the Ten Commandments and others more imposed by the religious hierarchy; However, this attachment to external practices, according to Jesus, is not enough to reach God. You need to open your heart to your neighbor with sincerity, without hypocrisy. Jesus rebukes the scribes and Pharisees: **"Woe to you, teachers of the law and Pharisees, you hypocrites! You shut the door of the kingdom of heaven in people's faces. You yourselves do not enter, nor will you let those enter who are trying to"** (Matthew 23:13)

The oldest monotheistic religion in the world, Zoroastrianism, founded by the Iranian prophet Zoroaster around 1600-1400 B.C. (depending on the sources used), has a unique importance in the history of religions not only because of its links with Hinduism, the major religion in India but also because it exerted a clear influence on the Abrahamic religions: Judaism, the Christianity, and Islam. Its code of moral conduct is based on three principles universally accepted by other religions: *good thoughts, good words, and good deeds*. Zoroaster called his religion or philosophy *"good conscience."* A Zoroastrian progresses toward God by his own choices: choosing to do good and avoiding to do evil. Zoroastrianism is sadly attributed to having introduced *dualism* into religions, creating in us a false sense of separation and estrangement from God.

All the world's major religions have the potential to serve humanity by establishing a code of moral conduct that enables a person who is doing evil to be transformed into a good person. But that benefit is minimal compared to the harm they have caused by *keeping the world in spiritual ignorance*. This lack of spirituality has contributed to the fact that, throughout history, religions have played a leading role in instigating wars and conflicts between human beings. Believers of the great organized religions, Christianity, Judaism, and Islam, which cover more than half of the world's population, have, for centuries, been killing each other for religious beliefs in the so-called "holy wars." No war can be holy. The conflict in the Middle East, in the Holy Land, between Jews, Christians, and Muslims, is one of the most complex, long-lived, and bloody in the history of humanity. Both are credited with that territory because it was "granted by God." These religions have shown a great narrowness of criteria and intolerance that have done enormous damage to humanity and have even taken the lives of millions of innocent people in God's name.

In Exodus 3:5, we read: **"For the place you are standing is holy ground."** If that observation were directed at a particular person, a nation, or a religion, it would be a sacrilege before God, but only because *God is omnipresence* that statement is ubiquitous a universal truth.

There is a phrase that sadly has gone down in history for the cruel and despicable, said by the papal legacy, Arnaud Amairic, in the crusade call against the Cathars in the 13th century. The Cathars practiced early Christianity, rejecting the mass, the sacraments, and the pope of Rome himself. They believed in reincarnation, they were vegetarians, and they rejected violence. That movement began in a small town in the south-west of France called Albi, and hence the name that is also given to the Cathars of "Albigenses." Pope Innocent III, considering the doctrines of the Cathars heretical, proclaims the crusade against the Albigensians who lived together with Catholics in the French city of Béziers. The chief of the crusaders besieged the city and, in the face of the Cathars' refusal to surrender, gave an order to take the city. Someone informed him that inside the city, there were also good Catholics who were not at fault. The leader of the crusades consulted with the papal legate Arnaud Amairic, who replied: *"Kill them all, that God will recognize his own."* This occurred on July 22, 1209. The number of casualties varies according to the sources, but it is estimated that some 17,000 men, women, and children, Cathars and non-Cathars, were stabbed to death.

Since the founding of Islam by the prophet Muhammad in the 6th century, there have been violent clashes by the leadership. After the prophet's death, there was a violent internal rupture, which continues to this day, represented by Iran (Shia) and Saudi Arabia (Sunni). In recent times, Islam has been corrupted by various interpretations practicing an extreme version of Islam, and there is no hesitation in shedding the blood of thousands of innocents in many parts of the world in the name of Allah.

In mid-August 2019, India and Pakistan turned 72 years old. Irreconcilable religious conflicts between Muslims and Hindus were the cause of partition of the vast Indian territory in August 1947 between Pakistan (Muslim) and India, despite their historical link. What was expected as an orderly separation ended in a violent exchange between those two religions that left at least one million dead and fifteen million displaced from their homes.

Dr. Deepak Chopra is right when he says that *"God gave the truth to man and the devil said: we are going to organize it and call it religion."* Organized religions have done humanity great harm by perverting the truth by teaching an external, humanized "God" who does not exist, to whom one must pray to obtain things. Most attention has been focused on enforcing man-made laws and regulations, observing rites, ceremonies, and creeds and demanding tithe to build churches to expand their political and economic power. They have forgotten the most important thing, which is to guide people in their spiritual realization. For this, they need to begin to teach mysticism as the only means of developing a spiritual consciousness and reaching God. *There is no higher religion than teaching the Truth.*

There is a great difference between religious life and spiritual life. The master Jesus revealed to the disciples what a spiritual life means: not to seek God in sacred mountains, cities or temples, but within oneself, not to do penance but benevolence, not to use rites, rituals, ceremonies or creeds, but to love your neighbor as yourself; consider our neighbor's children as our children; pray for our enemies; love the Lord, our God, with all our heart, with all our soul, and with all our mind; forgive seventy times seven; not to have anxious thoughts about what we are going to eat, drink or wear, but seeking the kingdom of God that is within us.

Unfortunately, the lesson has not yet been learned, as most people confuse a religious life with spiritual life. They naively think that, because they receive Communion every Sunday, they go to churches regularly and live a life without hurting anyone, they already have earned heaven. These religious people will be in for a great surprise when they make their transition to find out that there is no such God in heaven and that heaven is earth, as we will see in the next chapters. Undoubtedly, *spiritual ignorance* is our worst enemy.

2.6 GOD IS AN EXPERIENCE, NOT A BELIEF

Mystics tell us that God is an *experience*, not a belief or a concept, so it cannot be defined in words but *must be experienced.* The apostle Paul affirms, **"For the kingdom of God is not in words, but in power"** (I Corinthians 4:20).

One of the most profound truths in the Bible is that *knowing God is eternal life*. Remember what Jesus tells us in Matthew 22:32: **"God is not the God of the dead, but of the living."** And in John 17:3 he tells us: **"And this is life eternal: that they might know thee the only true God"**, and also, addressing the Jews who had believed in him, he said: **"And you shall know the truth, and the truth shall make you free"** (John 8:32). In this affirmation of Jesus, the Truth is synonymous with God, for what it would be equivalent to say: *"You shall know God, and God shall make you free,"* interpreting "knowing" in the sense of having the *experience* of God. And to have *the experience of God*, one must first understand ***the nature of God. The three great spiritual principles that must be indelibly impressed on your conscience are: omniscience, omnipotence, and omnipresence*** (Omni means "everything").

Omniscient means that God knows everything. If we have a God who knows everything and who loves us with infinite love, not only it is unnecessary to ask Him for peace in the world, for the destitute, for your family and friends and for yourself, but to do so is heresy, it is an insult to God. It is accusing God of not having enough love or enough power to meet our needs. It doesn't make sense to ask an infinite wisdom for something. Wisdom has to come from God to man, not from man to God. "God is," and we cannot expect God to change. The only thing we can ask God for is illumination. Our attitude should be to keep our ears attentive and to say in all humility: **"Speak, Lord, for your servant is listening"** (I Samuel 3: 9).

Omnipotence means that God can do it all, the almighty, absolute authority, infinite power, all the power there is, the only power. An infinite power and another additional power is not conceived. It is impossible! Omnipotence eliminates all other powers. There can be no other power in the universe. However, the human being gives power to the forces of evil even when none of those forces have power. It is only the universal hypnotism in which human consciousness is submerged that provides power to evil. We will talk about this extensively in the chapter "Man and his creation."

Omnipresence means that God is always present everywhere at the same time. Only an infinite God can be omnipresent. Consequently, being infinite is all that exists. Furthermore, **"God is Spirit"** (John 4:24), and **"That which is born of the Spirit is spirit"** (John 3: 6). Therefore, God has not been able to create a material world because

God is a Spirit, as we will see in Chapter 4 "Man and his creation." The Spirit is infinite, and, consequently, our real world is incorporeal and infinite, invisible to the human senses. You and I, and everyone else, are spirit and we are one with the Father now in this moment and always.

Omnipresence also means that God is present in hospitals, in prisons, on battlefields, in concentration camps, and in the Roman coliseum. However, God only becomes present in "this world" through the *enlightened consciousness of the individual.*

God is present! Certainly. Electricity has also been present through the ages, but what use has it been for humans in the past? None at all, because it had not been *realized*, made real, in the conscience of any scientist who expressed knowledge of electricity and the laws that govern it. The scientific consciences of Benjamin Franklin, Alessandro Volta, Thomas Edison, and others were required for humanity to benefit from the presence of electricity. The same can be said of the laws of aerodynamics, which have always been present and available to the human being. However, he had to wait until 1903, when the conscience of the Wright brothers was expressed in the construction and flight of the first plane.

God is present here and now, but in order to benefit from His Presence, God must be realized in the spiritual consciousness of some enlightened being so that His Presence is manifested externally in the form required at that moment. *That is the secret of spiritual life!* Repeating biblical quotes or metaphysical cliches should not be confused with *making God real in our conscience.* Those repetitions are as useless as if someone in Antiquity had said: "electricity is present." Yes, of course, it was available, but you did not have the knowledge to use it.

Until you make God something real in you, as real as your own body is for you, you will remain estranged from God like everyone who "have faith" in a "personal God" up there, who does not exist, and you will continue to sow in the flesh and reap corruption. **"God is omnipresence"**, and **"the kingdom of God is within you."** Not in sacred mountains, nor in sacred temples, nor in sacred books. And as the award-winning English poet Alfred Tennyson (1809-1892) says, *"He is closer to me than breathing, and nearer than hands and feet."*

In the end, we will all be taught by God, as Isaiah said: **"All thy children shall be taught by the Lord, and great shall be the peace of thy children"** (Isaiah 54:13). For now, let us honor God by realizing *His omniscience, His omnipotence, and His omnipresence.* Instead of asking God, let us seek silence within ourselves until we can hear **"A still small voice"** (I Kings 19:12). Then, we can say as the man born blind who was healed by God through the enlightened consciousness of Jesus: **"One thing I know, that, whereas I was blind, now I see"** (John 9:25).

CHAPTER 3

God and His Creation

3.1 THE MYSTERY OF GENESIS

The Bible is full of dualities and paradoxes that have confused theologians for hundreds of years. Fortunately, the mystics who have had the *experience of God* and communicate with the Almighty have clarified these apparent contradictions, as Biblical allegories and symbols cannot be deciphered intellectually, but spiritually. We use our intellectual powers to analyze or interpret the human experience but for spiritual things we need our *spiritual sense*, which reveals the hidden meanings that cannot be grasped by our human senses or by our mind. When Jesus rebuked his disciples, **"Having eyes, see you not? And having ears, hear you not?"** (Mark 8:18), he was referring to that inner vision and inner ear that mystics call *spiritual discernment* or *spiritual awareness*.

In the first book of the Bible, Genesis, which means beginning or origin, there are two versions of creation that are completely contradictory and conflictive, even though *Creation is one and only one, not two*. These two versions have remained next to each other for centuries, while theologians have tried with difficulty to reconcile the two versions without success. St. Jerome (343-420), Doctor of the Church and translator of the Bible into Latin, said, *"The most difficult and darkest of the sacred books, Genesis, contains as many secrets as it does words."* Those secrets are precisely what the mystics reveal to us in suggesting two different levels of consciousness that result in very different concepts about God, man and the universe. *This is so important and vital that until the world does not solve the mystery of Genesis, it will remain in the chaotic state in which it is now.*

3.2 SPIRITUAL CONSCIOUSNESS OR GOD

The first chapter of Genesis, from the mystical point of view, reveals the creation and activity of Spiritual Consciousness or God, who expresses Himself as a *spiritual universe* in which there is no conception or birth. It gives us an account of the development of the spiritual universe where light appears before the sun or the moon, the crops before the seeds have been planted, and the man before woman, *all by the work and grace of the Holy Spirit.*

"And God said, Let there be light, and there was light" (Genesis 1:3)

"And God said, Let us make man in our image, after our likeness" (Genesis 1:26)

"So God created man in His own image, in the image of God He created him; male and female He created them" (Genesis 1:27).

It should be noted that the spiritual interpretation that God "created them male and female" refers to the fact that the spiritual being has qualities of man and woman as complementary forces and not as opposing forces since one of the spiritual principles is *unity*. It is what in Taoism (Chinese mysticism) is known as yin and yang, apparently opposite or contrary forces but which are actually *complementary and interconnected*. That which is perceived as dual with yin and yang is actually an *indivisible whole*.

This first account of spiritual creation is the activity of that **Spiritual Consciousness** in all its purity and eternity. When Consciousness expresses itself as a spiritual form, it can appear as a seed, or as fully developed tree, or as spiritual being without having undergone any growth process.

The whole universe is a spiritual and infinite creation, it is not a physical or material and limited creation. According to the Bhagavad-Gita, the holy book of the Hindus, this material world that we humans observe, even with the help of scientific instruments, is only a fragment of what the spiritual universe is. *The material world is considered a partial reflection of reality*. It is like looking at the image of a tree in the clear waters of a river where the branches are on the bottom and the roots are on top. What we look at with our limited human senses is only a partial shadow of what is real, but from the shadows we can infer that something real exists.

Everything that is made by the **Spiritual Consciousness** is never born, for it is simply an expression or manifestation of that Consciousness which *has no beginning or end*. Time is not part of the spiritual creation; it simply does not exist. The eternal goes beyond time. *There is only now, The Eternal Now*. Time and space are concepts of the material world. We see and touch things that occupy three dimensions, and experience events in sequence, *but through* **spiritual discernment** *we grasp that the past, the present and the future are united in an eternal now*.

There is an interesting story from India about a man who conceptualizes time as he rafts down a river. In that moment, for him, it was the "here and now." As he goes downstream in his boat, he says the place he left behind was the past and where he is now is "here and now." Further downstream is the future and when he gets there, he finds that it is also "here and now." Therefore, if you could see the way that person appears from an aerial view above, you will find that what he calls the past, the present and the future are all present.

In the spiritual life there is only one time: now. The past glories as well as the past sins of our previous human lives do not count for our spiritual development, which is why we do not keep memory of it. The present is determined by our past actions, and the future by the present.

The present, "here and now," is the most important time in your life. Now is when you are living and where you can act. You cannot act either in the past or in the future, so focus your mind on *the present*. In the words of Ernest Hemingway (1899-1961), *"Today is only one day of all the days that will be, but what happens in all other days that come may depend on what you do today"* (For Whom the Bell Tolls). In other words, our future is but an extension of what we do in the present. The tomorrow that we will experience is an extension of our *current level of realized consciousness.* So if you want a future different from your present, change your *consciousness* to change your present.

3.3 THE ORIGEN OF THE UNIVERSE

The origin of the universe continues to be one of the greatest mysteries in science. There are various scientific theories about the origin of the universe, Einstein's theory of relativity being the most widely accepted. According to that theory, the universe was born approximately 10 to 20 billion years ago in a gigantic explosion called the Big Bang. All matter in the universe, including stars, galaxies, and planets, was originally concentrated in a super dense ball that exploded violently, creating our current expanding universe. However, no theory can explain what happened before the Big Bang or the original cause of it.

The mind or the intellect is the wrong tool to unveil the mysteries of God; to do so requires developing the faculty of *spiritual discernment*, which allows you to see what you cannot grasp with your mind, where the invisible, which is the real and eternal, becomes visible.

The apostle John, one of the greatest mystics of mankind, called the beloved apostle of Jesus for his elevated spiritual consciousness, offers us the eternal origins in the prologue of his Gospel: **"In the beginning was the Word, and the Word was with God, and the Word was God"** (John 1:1)

This revelation of the apostle John expresses the intimate union of the Word with God; the Word is the word and you cannot think without words. Try to think without words—you cannot. The word comes from the thought, and this in turn has its origin in the *Conscience*, which is expressed through the Mind. *Mind is the entrance and exit of Consciousness.*

In other words, what caused the divine Word was the *Spiritual Consciousness* or *God*, and while there is *Spiritual Consciousness*, that Conscience expresses itself in infinite spiritual forms—such as you and me, and like thousands of different species of trees, flowers, leaves, animals and minerals. If consciousness is not expressed it is *unconscious. Consciousness is always expressed in some way*, without any outside help.

Remember what the apostle Paul tells us in Hebrews 11:3, that *all that is visible is produced by what is invisible.* That invisible thing is specifically Consciousness or God. Consciousness is synonymous with God. If not for Consciousness, nothing would be expressed as a form or effect in the outside world, because *Consciousness or God is the creative principle and basic substance of life.* The apostle John is emphatic when he reveals to us that **"All things were made by Him, and without Him was not anything made that was made"** (John 1:3)

Metaphysicians and philosophers have interpreted the revelation of the apostle John on the origins of creation in a way that the mind identifies with God. However, the fact that we can *use* our mind is proof alone that the mind cannot be God because no one can use God. Moreover, the mind can be used for good or for evil, and that is another indisputable proof that it cannot be God. The mind is for the activity of reasoning and thinking. Consciousness does not think and or reason, it is simply and only consciousness. Consciousness cannot be manipulated. Consciousness just *is*. For example, when you have your husband or wife in front of you, you do not use your mind to know who you have in front of you, you are only *aware* of their presence. Also, you are *aware* of your own existence; you do not have to reason or think about that because feeling alive does not require a mental process. When the French philosopher René Descartes (1596-1650) said his famous phrase, "*I think, therefore I am*", he put the horse behind the cart. The truth is quite the opposite: *I am, therefore I think.*

3.4 CONSCIOUSNESS IS ONLY ONE

There is a *cosmic intelligence or cosmic energy that is infinite, eternal, omnipresent, omnipotent and omniscient,* which is the *Spiritual Consciousness* and that we call *God*. That is the Consciousness of the entire universe, without beginning and without end; and is in turn, our *individual consciousness* since being infinite also has to be One. The infinite cannot be infinity and then some. In fact, Consciousness, with capital C, or God is the only infinite that exists, because the infinite is not measurable or observable or limited in any way. It is not the mathematical concept of a never-ending quantity. *The Infinite*, properly speaking, *is all encompassing.*

Thus, Consciousness, being Infinite, is all that exists. We are all Consciousness and we are all in Consciousness. That is why the mystics speak of *the unity of being.* Consciousness, or God, *is* your being, my being and the whole universe. Just as gold is the substance that makes the ring, bracelet, necklace or any other form you want, God or Consciousness is the substance that constitutes the individual and everything else. God or Spiritual Consciousness is our life, our mind, our soul, our complete being, whether we are saints or sinners. To understand this better, visualize an immense Sun whose solar rays cover the entire infinite universe. Each ray of the Sun has the same qualities of the Sun, but it has nothing of its own, not even its own existence. So is our relationship with God. God is the life of the entire universe, and He created us as instrument for His expression. Do not forget our true identity: *we are spiritual beings created in the image and likeness of Spiritual Consciousness or God.*

Taking into account that everything that is visible is a manifestation or expression of the invisible and infinite Consciousness, we have to conclude that *everything is Consciousness.* In nature we find numerous examples that corroborate this truth. In the documentary "The March of the Penguins", it is observed that the penguins undertake a long walk in Antarctica every year, without maps or compasses to guide them, until they find a mass of ice thick enough to guarantee the safety of their young during the summer. How do the penguins know that? Is it their brain? No. It is the Consciousness that determines the sacrifice and love for their young, the amount of food to store in their bodies before embarking on their journey, the time of departure, the direction to follow, etc.

A very severe winter was forecast a few years ago in the eastern United States, based on the fact that the animals had developed thicker fur than usual and were storing more food than they used to. How can animals determine that? It is Consciousness that determines the thickness of their skin, the accumulation of fat and the amount of food to store. Birds and fish are also Consciousness and are in Consciousness. Otherwise, how can the migrations of the birds and the return of the fish to the places where they lay their eggs or spawn sites be explained?

Consciousness is the most important word in the vocabulary of mysticism, and is, in fact, the great Secret of Life. However, its meaning from the mystical standpoint, is as difficult to define as trying to define God, as

Consciousness in its purest form and God are synonymous. Conscience is God, and God is Consciousness.

When you say that you are in search of God, you are really in search of understanding what Consciousness is. Hindu mysticism defines God and man as follows:

"Man is an infinite circle whose circumference is nowhere, but the center is located in one spot; and God is an infinite circle whose circumference is nowhere, but whose center is everywhere. He works through all hands, sees through all eyes, walks on all feet, breathes through all bodies, speaks through every mouth and thinks through every brain. Man can become like God and acquire control over the whole universe, if he multiplies infinitely his center of self-consciousness. Consciousness, therefore, is the most important thing to understand."

Just as Consciousness is the most important word because God is Consciousness, the next most important word is *Love*: *unconditional, impersonal and universal. God is also Love. Consciousness is engaged with Love.* Jesus reveals it to us in Matthew 22:37-39 when he tells us that the greatest commandment of the Law is: **"To love the Lord thy God with all thy heart….and to love thy neighbor as thyself."** We become in tune with the Highest and become one with God only when unconditional, impersonal and universal Love is the animating principle of our existence. Note that it is unconditional, impersonal and universal Love that is considered Love from the spiritual point of view. It is not human love, which is for persons, family, an ethnic group or a country. In the words of Mahatma Gandhi (1899-1948) *"Love and Truth are the two faces of God, Truth is the end and Love is the way."*

3.5 CONSCIOUSNESS IS WHAT WE ARE

One of the greatest secrets of life is that we are all Consciousness, including God. We are not human beings, men or women, but *individual consciousness (consciousness with lower c)*. Now, there are stages and levels of consciousness, and this consciousness evolves individually and continues to expand until we reach the kingdom of God, because God is Spiritual Consciousness.

The Truth is that there is only one Being, only one Soul, only one Spirit, only one I, because God or Spiritual Consciousness is *infinite*. We are all ONE and the cause of all evil is the *perception of duality in our individual consciousness*. Not duality itself because if we were separate from God we would not exist since God is our life and the life of the universe. As soon as we *feel separate* from God and the universe, our problems begin.

The apostle John continues in the prologue of his gospel and confirms this unity when he tell us: **"And the Word was made flesh, and dwelt among us"** (John 1:14).

We, you and me, are the Verb made flesh. We are the Spiritual Consciousness expressing itself individually in spiritual form like you and me, but it is the expression of your *individual consciousness (consciousness with lower c)* that makes your body visible, of flesh and blood, and keeps your body standing, makes your heart beat and makes all the organs and cells of your body work. Your body is not solid as it seems. It is a union of molecules, cells and systems that are held together by the magnetic force of your individual consciousness. Your body would collapse if we remove your consciousness. If consciousness were not working in your body, your organs would be dead matter, without life. What, then, causes our organs and cells to function? Is it a God separated from us up there in the heavens or is it *the omnipresence of Consciousness or God* expressing Himself as your consciousness, my consciousness and as the whole life?

It is, precisely, this Consciousness that Jesus refers to when he tells us: **"The Father that dwelled in me, he does the works"** (John 14-10), or also when we read in the Scriptures: **"For the Lord your God go with you; he will never leave you nor forsake you"** (Deuteronomy 31:6). What can be with us through time, except our consciousness? The Master Jesus again refers to the Consciousness when he tells us: **"I and my Father are one"** (John 10:30). Certainly, we and the Consciousness of the Father are one. How could we be separated from the Spiritual Consciousness or God that is infinite, eternal and immortal, Creator of heaven and earth?

3.6 YOU ARE CONSCIOUSNESS

"Consciousness is What I Am" is the title of a book by mystic Joel S. Goldsmith (1892-1964); and that is precisely what we all are, including God.

The definition of consciousness that the dictionary gives us is: *"Your awareness of yourself and the world around you. This awareness is subjective and unique to you."* So how do you know that you are consciousness? Because you are aware of your own existence and your surroundings. You are aware of your body, you are aware of your family, you are aware of your profession or your work, you are aware of your friends, you are aware of the oceans, the stars, the sun, the moon, etc. Everything is included within your consciousness; if it were not in your consciousness, you could not be aware of it. This definition of consciousness corresponds to what mystics call *Mental Consciousness*, as we will see in the next chapter.

It should be clarified that our consciousness is not located in our body. The mystic Joel S. Goldsmith recommends that we do the following exercise. Start by thinking about your big toe and ask yourself: Is that me? The answer will come to you: "No, that's not me; that's mine." Now think about your foot to see if you are your foot or if the foot is yours. Continue with that question until you get to your head and see if you have been able to locate yourself in any part of your body. You will not find yourself in your body, because you are not there. *Your body is yours, but you are not in your body.* Why? Because *you are consciousness*.

Our consciousness expresses or manifests itself, among other things, as our bodies—but it is not *in* our body. No surgeon has ever found a consciousness embedded inside a body. To give an analogy, I am sure that as a child at your school you had a chance to move metal shavings placed on paper by moving a magnet below it, causing the shavings to appear to have lives of their own. Similarly, our body is kept alive by our *consciousness*. When Jesus tells us in Luke 17:21 that **"the Kingdom of God is within you"**, he is not referring to our body, because the finite cannot contain the infinite. He is speaking about *Consciousness*.

I must clarify that many neurologists, psychiatrists, scientists and philosophers use the terms brain, mind and consciousness indistinctly. That is a big mistake. The brain is an organ like any other organ of the human body, subject to deterioration due to time or illness. However, the fact that countless observations and clinical experiments have shown that certain specific areas of the brain correspond to memory, loss of language and functioning of some vital organs of the body, has led to some scientists to conclude that our minds and consciousness are intimately connected with the biological processes in our brain. That's like saying (to bring up an analogy) that a distortion on a TV screen due to bad operation of one of its transistors, and the replacement of those transistors to make it work again, are unequivocal evidence to conclude that the television is responsible of the programming that we see through it.

What's more, some neurologists, including a prominent professor and director of the Brain and Creativity Institute from the University of Southern California, claim to have located consciousness at the base of the brain (brain stem) and affirm that "consciousness is a state of mind and if there is no mind there is no consciousness." Consequently, we can infer that, when the brain dies, consciousness will also die. It is worth remembering what the Apostle Paul tells us in I Corinthians 2:14: **"But the natural man receive not the things of the Spirit of God, for they are foolishness unto him, neither can he know them because they have to be spiritually discerned."** The natural man is the human being, the prodigal son, the purely mental being who has the spiritual faculty asleep; that is to say, *the faculty of being able to see what is not evident to the mind.*

3.7 YOU ARE REALIZED CONSCIOUSNESS

The consciousness of the human being is entirely the Consciousness of God, but we have not realized that truth because of the *conditioning* that we have received in this life and in previous ones.

In English mysticism, there is a word to distinguish the infinite and unchanged Consciousness, or God, from human consciousness, which is *expanding* with our spiritual growth. That word is *awareness*. It is said, then, that human beings are *conscious awareness*, that is, we are *realized consciousness* or, what is the same, *we are what we have made real or realized in our consciousness.*

Everything that comes into our lives comes to us through what we have realized in our consciousness. If we have not realized in our consciousness the *omnipresence of God*, then we do not have it. If we have not realized in our conscience the *omnipotence of God*, then we don't have it. If we have not realized in our consciousness *the omniscience of God*, then we do not have it. In others words, we are all we can demonstrate at our current level of consciousness. We cannot demonstrate a level of consciousness that we have not reached.

It is important to take into account that human beings like you and me cannot pretend to live above our level of *realized consciousness* because it is very dangerous. A few years ago, a young Christian Science couple refused to take their baby with a very high fever to the hospital, thinking that they could lower his fever with meditation, and the baby passed away. They were tried and doomed. Obviously, that couple did not have the level of consciousness of spiritual healing required. There are frequent cases in which religious fanatics put their children's lives at risk by refusing medical treatment due to religious beliefs.

Being our Consciousness infinite, there are no limits on the demonstration of our consciousness. Yet we are the ones that put limits on this activity. For example, if you go to the ocean for a glass of seawater, you will return with a full glass of seawater, but if you go for buckets of seawater, you will return with buckets of seawater. The ocean is big enough to give you the amount you need. So with Consciousness, we can go there for a little or a lot, depending on the degree of development of Spiritual Consciousness that we have achieved.

Each of us is a unique representation of that "ocean of Consciousness." We are like the waves of an endless sea, and one of the purposes of living on this earthly plane is to give our individual conscience the opportunity to evolve into the infinite. Unfortunately we are born into a world where we learn to depend on individuals, governments and/or external things, and to seek happiness outside ourselves. We are never taught to depend on the Infinite Invisible of our Consciousness.

Our human consciousness is like the shutter of a camera. For a while it can accept very little light. But as we begin to spiritualize our consciousness, the shutter opens to admit more light, until eventually all the light passes through it.

As individual infinite Consciousness that we are, each one of us is a world in itself. The most important thing to know is that you, as you really are infinite Consciousness, *are the cause, not the effect*. *Our goal is to manifest, in its entirety, that Spiritual Consciousness or God.* But we can only demonstrate that which we have experience, not merely intellectual knowledge. We can attain that *experience* through *meditation*, a very important topic to be discussed in a separate chapter.

3.8 YOUR LEVEL OF REALIZED CONSCIOUSNESS DETERMINES THE QUALITY OF YOUR EXISTENCE.

The mystic Joel Goldsmith revealed the following spiritual principle: **"Nothing can happen to me that is not a reflection of my own level of realized consciousness."** That means that your outer life is a mirror of your inner life. In other words, all events in your life are the product of the contents of your individual consciousness, which is unique to you and only you can show. *That consciousness that is not in your body but that encompasses your entire universe: your body, your home, your business and all matters that concern you.*

It is the content of your consciousness (beliefs, feelings, emotions and thoughts) that governs all your activities. If you are going through a period of unhappiness, sickness, poverty, unrest and frustrations, remember that none of this has to do with your outer world, although you are sure the world 'out there' is to blame for your troubles. *Remember that all problems in your life have only one purpose: to offer you the opportunity to grow spiritually. There is no other reason.*

There is an apparently contradictory phrase of Jesus that says: **"Think not that I come to send peace on earth; I came not to send peace, but a sword"** (Matthew 10:34). The correct interpretation is that if you are enjoying a peaceful life with your family, maybe the best way to make you look for the true God is to disturb your tranquility; either with the loss of loved ones in an accident, an irreconcilable family conflict, a serious health problem, a financial crisis, the unexpected loss of a job or a new partner in your love life. Anything can happen to you. Of course God has nothing to do with that. Actually, as long as you are living as a human being, you are living your karma and it is your karma that, sooner or later, will bring you to your knees. If you could discern that the problems in your life are nothing more than a battle of your Christ or Spiritual Being that is trying to break through that hard and millennial crust that covers the material sense in which you were born, then you could win that battle.

The human being has realized in his *mental consciousness* that he is a creature separate and distinct from God, and, consequently, incapable to choose a spiritual life, that is, the true God. Hence the mystical meaning of the phrase of Jesus, when he tells us in the name of God: **"You have not chosen me, but I have chosen you"** (John 15:16).

About 1500 years B.C., a mystic revealed to us how his initiation was. He related all the problems to us, the discords and the vicissitudes he encountered on his spiritual path, and how such obstacles stood in the way of preventing him from reaching his demonstration of the Truth. He told us all the terrible trials and temptations that he had to overcome to finally reach its realization. In the end, he confesses that all this did not happen in the outside world but in his mind.

The enemy is within ourselves and it is *the conditioned mind of man*, a product of *universal hypnotism*, which is opposed to giving way to the Truth. Another mystic says: *"Stop looking victory over external conditions or persons, and allows the Christ in you ascend so that the light reveals that there is no such darkness."*

Indeed, at some point in our lives the *Christ or Spirit of God within us* makes its way and from that very instantly our spiritual growth is determined. It does not matter how long or how many lives it takes, no matter how rebellious or how stubborn we are to properly interpret the message that we are receiving, since infallibly the moment will come when we will stop "sleeping with the pigs" and begin the way to the House of the Father or Spiritual Consciousness. **"As I live, says the Lord, every knee shall bow to me, and every tongue shall confess to God"** (Romans 14:11).

I must clarify that the phrase of Jesus mentioned above; **"I have not come to send peace on earth, but a sword"**, has been interpreted erroneously by some religious hierarchs to authorize the force in spreading the Christian faith. In the evangelization of the natives of America, the cross always accompanied the sword. All those impositions of the Christian faith forcibly contradict the teachings of the master Jesus, who tells us: **"Blessed are the peacemakers, for they shall be called the children of God"**(Matthew 5: 9); **"Do not resist evil"**(Matthew 5:39); and also **"Love your enemies and bless them that curse you"** (Matthew 5:44).

Definitely, what you accept or reject in your *consciousness* is what determines what you are and what you will be. How many people have the courage to accept the fact that the failures in their life are owe exclusively to themselves? Very few, surely. *Our external experience is the reflection of the content of our own consciousness.* And never forget that, because you're going to save yourself years of misery blaming others for your problems, when the only one responsible for them is you.

But the important thing is not the problems themselves, but how we react to the problems we face in our lives. There is a popular saying that says: *"Every cloud has a silver lining."* Evil is not our enemy, it is our way of reacting to evil what is decisive. I have witnessed people who were faced with serious personal problems or the loss of loved ones, have grown spiritually, and others who, faced with similar problems, have used them as excuses to continue sinking into the human mud, and some have gone to the extreme of taking their own lives.

There is a Buddhist proverb that says: **"Every human being is given the key to the gates of heaven; the same key opens the doors of hell."** You, and only you, choose where you want to live. *We create our own reality.*

You are solely responsible for what happens to you! Your life depends exclusively on you. The mirror of your life is in front of your own face. In life there is no chance. Nothing is random but our ego refuses to accept it and will always find an external reason to blame. Careful with that! Whatever happens, there is always a deeper reason. *Transform your consciousness, and everything changes!*

That spiritual principle that Joel Goldsmith has revealed to us is also supported by another universal law, which is **the law of attraction** that says that **the similar attracts the similar**. That is to say, that you attract to your life that which is in vibrational resonance with you. Actually, it's just another way of expressing *the law of cause and effect or karma*, which operates only at the level of human or *mental consciousness*.

In the United States, a book and a video called *The Secret* were released, which is the metaphysical interpretation of the *law of attraction*. It has been widely accepted for the powerful and, at the same time, simple message that states that you can be the master of your own destiny if you think positively. However, many people complain that they do not obtain the expected results, because their wishes never materialize. The reason is that a few positive thoughts are not going to change your whole belief system and the way you act and think that are so ingrained in your subconscious through many of your previous lives. You have to live daily with those new thoughts for a long time so that they can settle into your mental consciousness, which is what is going to express itself externally. Many people do not have the patience and perseverance required to that. It should be noted that this method, The Secret, is purely mental, there is nothing spiritual about it.

To the extent that you spiritualize your conscience, with spiritual readings like these and with spiritual thoughts, to that same extent will external changes occur in your life. How wonderful it is to know that, for eternity, whatever need you have will be covered by the unfolding of your own consciousness, and that that unfolding will never depend on the outside world! Your Consciousness is the point of contact between you and your source. *The kingdom of God in its entirety is within your own consciousness!*

Our level of consciousness determines the plane of existence in which we live. When we live on a material level of consciousness, ignorant of our spiritual nature, our level of vibration is very low. At that level we are what the apostle Paul calls "*the natural man,*" whose first instinct is survival and for whom the end justifies the means. On that level of *mental consciousness*, where we are able to run over others in order to save our ego or ensure our physical or economic survival, we can be victims of anything: murder, kidnapping, rape, serious accidents, wars, plague, famine, etc.; anything is possible and we can experience it since, at that level, we are just statistics. Similarly, the reason why we can come to this world with a physical or mental defect is that we are born in a state of spiritual ignorance.

As we begin to *spiritualize our consciousness*, our level of *realized consciousness* begins to rise, and gradually we are elevated to another plane of existence of higher vibrations. At that level there is no longer, for us, murder or rape, but we can be victims of lesser evils such as divorce, envy, hatred, disease, poverty, etc. As we continue to grow spiritually, we move on to another plane of existence where we harbor great anxiety or fear of death or illness or accidents or being poor; and so, we gradually continue to learn lessons that help us go gradually discovering the Truth. One can pass through several planes of existence in a single life, depending on our spiritual growth.

Furthermore, the plane of existence into which we are born depends on the level of consciousness reached in previous lives. We choose those parents whose combined level of vibrations is equal to ours. So never blame your parents for your ills, since it has been your level of consciousness of that moment that has attracted those parents to you; and if they weren't called Maria and Juan, they would be Corina and Rafael, but they are the ones who would provide you with the environment required by you at the level of your realized consciousness of that moment.

3.9 CONSCIOUSNESS AFTER DEATH

I am the consciousness that gives life to this body and at the moment in which I detach myself from this body, I immediately form another body in a world less dense than the material world, with higher vibrational frequency, invisible to human eyes that is the *astral world*; but it's always me, *consciousness*. And I am also *expressed consciousness*, because I could not exist unless I express myself. What would become of me if I couldn't express myself in this world or in any other? Nothing!

Everything, absolutely everything, the visible and the invisible to our senses, is in Consciousness. Nothing, absolutely nothing, is found out of the infinite and omnipresent Consciousness, not even what our very limited physical senses consider the "other side" or "the afterlife."

What the world calls *death* does not mean a change in consciousness. By making the transition, you will not be better or worse than you already are at present. Your level of consciousness will remain the same as it is now. This has been confirmed in several experiments made in communication with the spirits of the dead. The contacted spirits maintained the same interests and tastes as they had as human beings. So if someone contacted you once that you have made your transition, you will probably answer the same way as when you were in visible form. Your level of consciousness won't show any change, unless you've advanced on your spiritual path here on earth; then yes, by making your transition, your spiritual advancement will be much greater.

For people with spiritual knowledge, what the common people call "death" is nothing but the transition from one experience to another experience. It's like going from infancy to puberty, then puberty to early maturity, and so on, without having to die for it. *Death is, simply, a gradual process of spiritual growth.*

Now, the *astral world* is not heaven where many religious and good people think they go after death. These people think that because they have done no harm to anyone, they have gone to mass weekly, they have received communion regularly and have contributed to the works of the Church, they are free of sin and when they die, they will meet God in heaven. These people are going to be in for a big surprise when they make their transition because they will find themselves in an *invisible human world* at a *lower level of consciousness* than when they left, and they will continue to pay karma, life after life, as long as they believe in a fake God separated and different from them.

The afterlife aspect of Christian doctrine was masterfully captured by the Franciscan poet Dante Alighieri (1265-1321) in his work the *Divine Comedy*, considered a masterpiece of world literature, where he narrates in the form of a poem a history of the afterlife divided in three parts: "Hell", "Purgatory" and "Paradise", which is the heaven. Dante shows a great power of synthesis, typical of the great poets, but whose vision is limited by their own doctrine religious and by the time and place where he lived.

Mystics do not mention the *astral world* because for them it is another *mental world*, invisible to the human senses, and like the earthly world, it is yet another *illusion. It is also maya*! To learn about that world you have to go to the occult, which is the study and the practice of occult sciences or paranormal phenomena. That is not in our interest, because it is not necessary for our *spiritual development*, which is *the only way to reach God*.

However, achieving control of your mind in this human life will be very helpful to you in the astral or "ghosts" world, as some call it, because being a less dense world your thoughts will be expressed instantly. According to occultists, the astral world consists of seven planes of existence and these, in turn, have seven subdivisions, and so on until the seventh grade. These planes do not lie one above the other in space but interpenetrate at the same point in space because they are different energy levels that correspond to the different levels or stages of consciousness. There is an ancient aphorism which says: *"A plane of existence is not a place but a stage of being."*

3.10 QUESTIONS AND ANSWERS

- Can a disabled or troubled baby be born into a spiritual family?

The answer is yes, of course. Our human life is one life of interrelations and is, precisely, the problems derived of those interrelations that force us to look for spiritual solutions. There is no way to grow spiritually unless we have problems or (as the mystic Barbara Muhl calls them) "needles" and many times those "needles" are the ones we marry or give birth to, or we find them with our own parents or relatives. Thus, a disabled child can arrive to a spiritually alert family, but their vibration level would be equal to the parents. However, that would be the experience for which those parents and/or son or daughter would have to pass to continue their spiritual growth.

- Why would a couple who genuinely loves each other and wants to stay together, have a lousy relationship full of misunderstandings and disputes where they hurt each other to the point of ending their relationship?

The answer is that every person who comes into our lives is a reflection of some aspect of ourselves, of our unique set of experiences and perspectives. So much so that all the people who have crossed your path, both the ones you like and the ones you dislike, are a mirror of the content of your consciousness and have served to reinforce your belief system in a kind of a vicious circle that is very difficult to break. And, without exception, *are showing you something you need to spiritually correct in your life*. Never forget that whatever the qualities you are looking for in a partner, those qualities are not found in the air or anywhere else but in your own consciousness. You should bring those qualities into your consciousness first, because we externalize in our lives the content of our conscience. And if you do not achieve a change of consciousness in this life, you will continue in your next lives with that same problem, each sharper and sharper, until, one day, tired of so much pain, like the prodigal son, you will bend your knees before the Lord. The human solutions such as going to a couples counselor or anger management therapies can help you control your behavior, but not your thoughts, which will remain the same and will continue to create karma. *The only solution is the spiritualization of your consciousness.* Upon achieving this, your partner automatically changes or is removed from your life.

The mystic Barbara Muhl tells us in her work *Script, Kid and Fantasyland* that when we react disproportionately or violent in front of a person who has told us something, it is because that person "has perfectly read our script." The magnetic power of that script of our life, which we have written ourselves in ignorance, is so strong that we are magnetically attracted to certain people, places and experiences. That is, it is the content of our consciousness, product of experiences that we have had in our current and previous lives, which creates the events that reinforce our beliefs and what connects us to people who read our script without even trying to do so, or be aware of it. It is a classic example in where the *"similar attracts the similar."* Human life is a kind of vicious circle in which we get trapped due to our *spiritual ignorance*.

Let's not forget that karma, or law of cause and effect, is what takes care of providing us with problems, over and over again, until we finally manage to resolve them spiritually. Once we learn to spiritually manage that particular problem, we are forever free from it; it will never appear in our lives again. The reason that it takes us time and effort dissolving that specific problem is that we have many lives going in the opposite direction, by accepting the lies of the world. *Keep in mind that this world is the great school to which we all come to learn to spiritualize our conscience.*

-When making the transition, do we meet again with the people we love?

The answer is yes, of course. Love is a feeling that when it is mutual it keeps us together for eternity. If we want it and if they want it too, so it will be. As long as there is a mutual correspondence, that union will remain. We have relatives in this world that we never meet and, sometimes we don't want to see them either. But if you have someone in your heart and in your soul here on earth, you can rest assured that that person, who feels the same for you, is going to be with you on your travels here on earth or if you pass into a new existence. One never lets their loved ones get out of their heart, soul and mind. And if they love you too, that seals the union forever both here and in the "hereafter."

-To the question of why do bad things happen to good people?

The answer is given by the Apostle Paul, in Galatians 6:8: "**For he that sow to his flesh shall of the flesh reap corruption.**" It does not matter that we are a good human being, that we do no harm to anyone, that we fulfill our duties as father or mother and that we go to church every Sunday. If we put our faith in money, in political influences or in a God "out there", we are sowing to the flesh and we will reap discord and disharmony. We have already pointed out that the Jesus Christ told the Jews that being a good Hebrew was not enough to enter the kingdom of heaven. Ignorance in spiritual matters it is not a mitigating factor before the law of **"Whatsoever a man sow, that shall he also reap"** (Galatians 6:7). Good people in this life create good karma with their actions and possibly will have more good things that bad, but it is not under the protection of God. *The solution is to spiritualize our conscience to get to know our true spiritual identity.*

The Law of Attraction explains this apparent contradiction between bad things and good people, as follows: our predominant level of vibration is formed by all that environment where we are born and develop, and we attract into our lives that with which we are in vibrational resonance. For instance, if we are born in a country where people are starving, the reality that we perceive is the lack of food. We learn this at an early age through our parents and the environment that surrounds us, and therefore, we produce a very low level of vibration, which is transmitted from generation to generation, and that corresponds to the vibration level of that country. People are not to blame because, in general, it is an unconscious act that keeps those people in a vicious cycle of poverty, difficult to break regardless of whether they are mostly good people. *The solution is still a change in people's level of realized consciousness.*

3.11 ALL THINGS WERE MADE BY GOD

The apostle John, referring to Creation, continues in the prologue of his gospel saying: **"All things were made by Him; and without Him was not anything made that was made."** (John 1:3).

According to the Vedas, the basis of Hindu religion, the Creation and the Creator are two parallel lines without beginning or end. There could *never have been a time when Creation did not exist.* In other words, everything that exists was created by God simultaneously from the very beginning of Creation, since you cannot have God separate from its Creation, just as Creation cannot have a time after God. God and his manifestation had to be simultaneous and instantaneous.

God is the *causative principle* of the universe, but we cannot say that God created the universe, because that would imply that there was a time when God existed and the universe did not. As well as, for example, you can't have created the math principle and then made 2x2=4, or the principle of chemistry and then make H_2O=water; that had to be simultaneous and instantaneous.

On the other hand, *God made His Creation complete from the very beginning and nothing new has ever been added to His Creation.* The Scripture tells us, **"For I am the Lord, I change not"** (Malachi 3:6). Each particle of the universe is in constant motion and change in relation to other particles. All that is finite, like ours body, our mind, our planet earth, our galaxy, changes continuously, but taking the infinite universe in its entirety, this cannot change. To say that *infinity* somehow undergoes changes is absurd. Movement is always relative in relation to something else. Consequently, the *infinite Creation* is absolute, immovable, unchanged, without beginning or end, from eternity to eternity, because you cannot have a beginning without having an end, and vice versa.

3.12 ALL GOOD THINGS COME TO US FROM GOD

In Genesis 1:31 it reads: **"And God saw everything that He had made, and, behold, it was very good."** That means, everything that God created was very good. To this we can add that all good things come to us from God. Jesus confirms this concept when he says: **"Why do you call me good? There is none good but one, that is, God"** (Mark 10:18).

As long as you think that you are good, that you are generous, that you are moralist, that you are benevolent, that you are upright, that you are religious, that you are a good father or mother, that you are prosperous, you are a prodigal son. It is giving credit to your personal ego that immediately separates you from God. That is not giving up your individuality since it becomes greater as we give way to the infinite qualities of God. We are an instrument that reflects the qualities of God. In our *spiritual ignorance,* we have been victims of *universal hypnotism* that make us act in the wrong way, submitting ourselves to the law of Cause and Effect or karma that is not really a law; it is just *the belief in our consciousness that we are separated from God. It is impossible to be separated from God because we would not exist.*

If human beings show good qualities, we recognize those qualities as the activity of God expressing Himself through us. Humans cannot understand this because by looking at us with their human eyes we are good or bad. However, through our Spiritual Consciousness we can *spiritually discern* the goodness of the Father expressed in each one of us. God is the only creative principle of the universe. Due to the infinite nature of God, there is only one Life, one Soul, one Spirit, one Law, one Creator, even one Body, and that is God. To understand this better, visualize a Tree of Life that covers the entire universe. God is the Tree of Life and each one of us is one of its branches. You are a branch and I am another branch, regardless of color, race or religion to which we belong or do not belong. When we look at the Tree with its trunk, roots and branches we see a Tree, a form, a body. We do not believe that each branch has its own body. There is a body, the body of the Tree, and the body of the Tree includes everything from the roots to the most extreme tip of each branch. We are branches of the Tree of Life that encompasses the entire universe. *And God is the force that gives life to the Tree of Life.*

In this human, materialistic world, we falsely consider ourselves as individual beings separate from each other and separate from God, and we think that what affects me does not affect you. They are those who even believe that they can deprive others of something for their own benefit. *That is totally false, all an illusion.* In the Tree of Life, any benefit or harm, benefits or harms us equally. **"Inasmuch as ye have done it unto one of the least of these my brethren, ye have done it unto me"** (Matthew 25:40).

The apostle John is emphatic when he reveals that **"All things were made by Him; and without Him was not anything made that was made."** (John 1: 3). There has been no more creation after this. There is only one creator and to accept that evil exists is to believe in another creator. God never created a power to destroy his creation. **"I am the first, and I am the last; and beside me there is no God"** (Isaiah 44:6). God has no enemies. God has no opponents. *God is omnipotent, omnipresent and omniscient.* So what can exist except God? Nothing! There is only God. Nothing else exists. In the words of the greatest American poet and very spiritual person, Walt Whitman (1819-1892), *"I don't know anything that isn't a miracle."* That is, everything is spiritual. And, said by Albert Einstein (1879-1955), *"There are only two ways to live your life. One is as though nothing is a miracle. The other is as if everything is a miracle."* Being infinite, God is everything. It could not be otherwise. All that God is, God was; all that God was, God is now; all that God is now, God will be forever.

If you have an Invisible Infinity you cannot have that and something else because you destroy the Infinite, and that means that you have destroyed your God. The moment you think that there is "God and something else" you are destroying your God; as for example, "God and man" or "God and evil" or "God and the universe" or "God and me."

Nevertheless, the entire world has been brought up, by every religious teaching, to believe that there are two powers and that we could make contact with the power of good to overcome the power of evil. However, the founder of Christianity taught us more than two thousand years ago to **"Resist not evil"** (Matthew 5:39). But the belief in two powers is so ingrained in us, that we find it almost impossible to believe that there are no other powers. A change in consciousness is necessary in order to understand and accept the radical teaching of Jesus Christ.

3.13 GOD CREATED A SPIRITUAL UNIVERSE

Creation, the one and only true Creation, is the immaculate conception of God or Spiritual Consciousness revealing itself as individual identity. An Identity expressed in Spirit in infinite ways. *You, I and all beings and all animate and inanimate things are spirit, eternal and immortal.*

This concept is of paramount importance for your spiritual development and should be very clear in your mind. *Creation is only one and is spiritual.* The truth about this world we live in is that everything is spiritual. It could not be otherwise because, as Jesus tells us, **"God is spirit"** (John 4:24) and **"that which is born of the Spirit is spirit"** (John 3:6). In other words, *God could not create a material universe, because God is Spirit.*

That eternal, immaterial, spiritual and infinite Creation, invisible to human senses and that can only be captured by our spiritual sense is the real, true, unique Creation, where God or Spiritual Consciousness is the essence and substance of all things. Even what appears as stone, sand, soil, as well as that same Consciousness itself is our own identity, since we were created by God in His image and likeness to have dominion over everything upon the earth, forever and ever.

In the real spiritual world, created by God, everything is happiness, harmony and abundance. There is no pair of opposites but only unity, and the only power is the infinite, impersonal and universal love of God. It is the spiritual paradise where the sheep sleep with the lions and where all our needs, as well as those of the animals, vegetables and minerals are covered by the grace of God or Spiritual Consciousness. It is the kingdom of God that Jesus refers to when we He says, **"My kingdom is not of this world"** (John 18:36). If at any time we perceive that the creation in any of its forms (animal, vegetable or mineral) expresses some evil, that it is but the reflection of the level of *collective realized consciousness of the human being,* as we will see in the next chapter.

Biblical historians estimate that this first chapter of Genesis was written many centuries after the second and third chapter, perhaps around 500 years B.C. It is obviously the revelation of a mystic who achieved complete union with God. Its authorship is assigned to the first of the major prophets, the great Old Testament mystic: Isaiah. Without a doubt, the level of Isaiah's consciousness is far above the level of consciousness of those who wrote the next two chapters of Genesis that we will see next.

CHAPTER 4

Man and his creation

4.1 MENTAL CREATION

The second chapter of Genesis radically differs from the first. In this second chapter, God does not create man and woman in His image and likeness, but forms man from the dust of the earth and woman from man's rib.

"And the Lord God formed man of the dust of the ground" (Genesis 2:7). **"And the rib, which the Lord God had taken from man, made He a woman"** (Genesis 2:22).

And from the oldest book in the Bible, Job says to God: **"Remember that thou has made me as the clay; and wilt thou bring me into dust again?"** (Job10:9).

In ancient times, man used to make clay statuettes representing various gods, such as gods of fertility, rain, war, and others, so it was natural to consider God as a potter who formed man out of clay. *That dust of the earth, according to the mystics, is nothing other than the mind of the human being.*

The creation described in the second and third chapters of Genesis is not a spiritual and eternal creation of God, but a material and mortal creation of the mind of man. In our human world the mind is the essence of creation.

Our world is a mental world in which the mind is the substance that constitutes or forms all the material things that you see around you. The mind functions as thought and the energy generated by that thought appears as material objects. The material world that we perceive with our senses is a mental world. It is the mental creation of the second chapter of Genesis; of the mind that believes in the power of good and in the power of evil.

In our human world, the outward appearance is always formed by the mind. An example that would help us better understand this concept is the combination of two hydrogen atoms and one of oxygen to form a water molecule. The water molecule can be water or transformed into vapor or ice. However, water, vapor and ice are just different frequencies of vibration or different forms of a single essence: two parts of hydrogen and one of oxygen. Another example is considering the mind as a mold for cakes where the cake would be the matter, which takes the form of the mold, which is the mind.

Mind is the basic substance of the entire physical world and matter is the name given to the mind when it takes shape. For example, the mind in the human body can appear in many forms: flesh, blood, bones, organs, etc., but each of these parts is nothing more than the mind at a very low vibration frequency that makes it visible to the human eye, appearing in a specific way, but always the basic substance or essence is the mind.

As human beings, we all have a physical body and a mind, and what we mentally sow is what we go to reap in our material world. That is nothing other than the law of cause and effect or karma in action that we have mentioned before and which in Christian mysticism is known as that law that **"Whatsoever a man soweth, that shall he also reap"** (Galatians 6:7). As human beings, our body is under physical law and our mind under mental law. And so it will be until we achieve the Grace of God or Christ or Spiritual Consciousness, where karma no longer operates.

The physical law of the body is *"rest, nutrition and exercise."* The three aspects are of equal importance. Note that "sleep" is not mentioned but "rest." From the mystical point of view, "sleep" is not an activity of God. It's the closest to being unconscious and it is only necessary for the universal beliefs of the human being. A large percentage of the adult population takes drugs to combat insomnia, with a whole sequel of side effects, when the important thing is to rest, which is achieved simply by laying horizontally on the bed or on the floor, neutralizing the effect of gravity on the body and filling our minds with spiritual truths. Regarding nutrition and exercise, you have to stay informed of the latest scientific advances in these matters and put them into practice.

The mental law, as we shall see later, is that a mind absent of errors and saturated with spiritual principles is a blessing for you and for all the people around you and it is what leads us to reach an unconditioned, transparent mind, which is what allows the spiritual consciousness to express itself in a harmonious way. We achieve that mind with our dedication and practice of spiritual principles in our daily life.

The Bible refers, in an allegorical way, to the cause of the *mental creation* of the human being as the original sin that caused the expulsion of Adam and Eve from Eden. That sin was neither the apple nor sex, as some of the traditional religions do identify it, but rather *the acceptance in our consciousness of knowledge of good and evil.*

"Of every tree of the garden you may freely eat; but of the tree of the knowledge of good and evil, you shall not eat of it: for in the day that you eat, you shall surely die" (Genesis 2:16-17).

The symbolic figures of Adam and Eve represent the human race who accepted in their conscience the belief in those two powers, the power of good and the power of evil. These powers are represented in their two sons, Cain and Abel: one bad and one good. *By the human being accepting this belief in his consciousness, a false sense of separation from God was realized.* That was the birth of the personal sense or ego (the me, me and mine, mine) and the beginning of judging people and things as good or bad, which makes us experience separation rather than unity with God.

When the human being *feels separated* from the Conscience-God, they fall in deep degradation, with crime and murder becoming natural companions of a very low level of consciousness, and from that moment the Mind, instead of being a pure instrument of God or Spiritual Consciousness, becomes the *conditioned mind* of the man who begins to create material forms of good and evil. The human race then fell into what is symbolically known as the *"Adam's dream"*, because he is asleep, dreaming that he is separated and estranged from God. **"And the Lord God caused a deep sleep to fall upon Adam, and he slept"** (Genesis 2:21).

In other words, *the greatest sin of us human beings has been accepting in our conscience the egocentrism and the powers of good and evil*, and from that moment on we condemn ourselves forever to earn a living through the sweat of our forehead, to give birth in pain and to live in a world of pairs and opposites: harmony and discord, poverty and abundance, disease and health, births and deaths.

But at no time can we hold God responsible for that. Do you realize how "inhuman" the "God" of the second creation was presented to us by the Bible? How many times would a mother forgive her child for disobedience? However, that "God" has been relentless not only with Adam and Eve, who were ultimately the ones who committed original sin, but also with all their descendants. That is a tremendous injustice, even judging that "Divine decision" by human standards. It is simply absurd and blasphemous to attribute this creation to God, one of whose attributes is precisely infinite, impersonal and universal love towards all his children.

Do you believe that God and human suffering can exist? Do you think that there may be children suffering before the indifferent gaze of God? If we as human parents would never allow a child to get sick, if we could help it. *Do you think God would allow wars and cruelty between human beings?* Of course not! There's no such thing! *That "God" created by the unenlightened mind of the human being does not exist!*

God does not do evil nor is He responsible for suffering in this material world. God is not even aware of it. People generally think that God knows our every thought and even the number of hairs on our head, wanting to say that God is intimately involved in our lives. That is true from a spiritual point of view, but it is not true in the material world we live in. Remember what Jesus tells us, that **"God is Spirit"** (John 4:24) and **"That which is born of the Spirit is spirit"** (John 3:6). In other words, *God has not been able to create a material world because God is Spirit*.

Therefore, that creation mentioned in the second and third chapter of Genesis is not from God. And also because: **"All things were made by**

Him and without Him was not anything made that was made"(John 1: 3) and because: **"And God saw everything that He had made, and, behold, it was very good"** (Genesis 1:31). Consequently, that creation is fictitious, it is a lie, it is not real, it does not exist before God. *It only exists in the conditioned mind of human beings.* It is the false world of the senses, of deceptive mental images of reality, of mirages formed by the mind of man that have no real existence. However, it must be recognized that, despite the fact that human beings are living only a bad dream, we suffer physically and we feel pain. *But the only way to free yourself from the terror of a nightmare is waking up.*

4.2 OUR FIVE SENSES AND OUR MIND DECEIVE US

Our sense of sight captures an ever-changing world: a world of babies, young people, adults and the elderly, of sick people and healthy people, rich and poor, happy and unhappy, the living and the dead. All these are but *mental images* that make our existence a *mental experience*, and since there is only *one mind*, it is the mental image that your mind and mine capture. *That world of mental images has no real existence.*

The human being is an illusion, but underneath that illusion is the "real man" (God personified*). It is impossible to be separated from God because we would not exist.* I repeat what the apostle John revealed to us in John 1: 3: **"All things were made by Him and without Him was not anything made that was made"**; it happens that with our human eyes, with our mind, we cannot see God's creation.

I will give you an example to try to better explain this difficult concept. If you go out tonight to look at the stars, it will seem that the earth and all the stars are totally immobile. However, everything is spinning at astonishing speeds. The floor where you are standing is turning on itself at a speed of 1,675 kilometers per hour, while moving around the sun (translational movement) at the speed of 107,000 kilometers per hour. That is nothing compared to the galactic rotation spinning at 810,000 kilometers per hour. However, the perception of our mind, interpreting what our senses capture, is that our floor and the entire star system are immobile. It is commonly said that "perception is reality", but it is only reality in the minds of individuals who perceive it as real, because externally it does not exist.

Those mental images that make us take appearances for realities only take place in people's minds. In the same way, the mirage in the desert is a mental image that does not exist outside the mind; it is a false perception of what you are looking at. Likewise, when you look at the horizon, there is no such horizon. When you watch the railroad join in the distance or when you look at the sun spinning around the earth, all of those are just optical illusions that are only in your mind, but they are not real because the illusion cannot be externalized.

This was clearly grasped by some philosophers of the seventeenth century, like the French René Descartes (1596-1650) and the English John Locke (1632-1704), who argued that our understanding of the reality ultimately depends on what we experience through our *unreliable five senses*.

Galileo Galilei (1564-1642) changed his view of the universe by increasing his sight with a rudimentary telescope. That allowed him to perceive a universe different from that of the accepted theory at that time when the sun and the other planets revolved around the earth. It should be noted that his support for Copernicus' heliocentric theory earned him a life sentence from the Holy Inquisition. He was saved from being burned at the stake by his humiliating retraction.

Plato (427-347 BC), in his famous Allegory of the Cave, in Book VII of The Republic, presents to the Western world his concept that the world that we grasp with our senses is not real but a poor copy of the real one. Compare the appearances of our world with shadows of real things projected on the walls of a cave in which we are immobile prisoners who look at the shadows and we create the illusion that the shadows are the real things.

This concept of Plato is not original at all. Many years before him, one of the greatest mystics of all time and without doubts the greatest of India, Gautama the Buddha, revealed to the world, 550 years BC, that *the material world* that we *perceive* with our senses is *maya or illusion*. That is an absolute truth and one of the greatest revelations that the human being has received, only comparable to that of Moses when God revealed his name to him: *"I am"*, and with that of Jesus who showed us that God is *love* and for the first time the message of *love* was revealed to the world.

Jesus gives us a message identical to that of Buddha when he tells us in John 18:36: **"My kingdom is not of this world."** In other words, Jesus is telling us that the world he lives in is not this mental world of the human being, plagued by scarcity, limitations, sickness and death, but the real immortal world of God. That is the reason why Jesus in the Sermon on the Mount commands us: **"Resist not evil"** (Matthew 5:39), because all evil is illusion. You do not fight the mirage in the desert, the horizon in the distance or the water on the freeways on a sunny day, you just ignore them. The mystic does not fight the evil that he encounters on his way, but *realizes the presence of God in his conscience so that evil dissolves like darkness before light.*

Thus, *God's creation is spiritual, immaterial, and infinite* but it is perceived by our mind as material, physical and limited. The reason for this anomaly is that our mind, in its unenlightened state, interprets for us what we grasp with our very limited five senses and consequently it is a distorted and false interpretation of reality. In the same way, quantum physics shows us that the chair in which you are sitting and all the material world around us is not solid but a field of energy in motion, which is mostly empty space but gives us the illusion of solidity.

4.3 DO NOT JUDGE BY APPEARANCES

Now you can understand why regardless of the appearances (whether good or bad), Jesus' answer was always: **"Judge not according to the appearance"** (John 7:24). Indeed, we should not believe what we see or hear with our deceitful senses because, apart from being just an illusion, judging by the appearances we set karma in motion, immediately separating ourselves from God.

No one can identify with their true spiritual self while judging by appearances, because the human mind with which he is judging is in a hypnotic state. Our duty is to develop our faculty of *spiritual discernment*, which is what allows us to see through appearances, good and bad, and not fall into temptations.

Jesus, in his *spiritual discernment*, realized in his conscience the *omnipotence of God*, that is, that God is the only power that exists regardless of the illusory nature of the errors. The Lazarus' resurrection allowed Jesus to demonstrate to a crowd that death has no power, despite appearances, and that life is indestructible because it is created by God. Unfortunately, two thousand years later, human beings are still in a state of denial of what was revealed and demonstrated by Jesus.

There is a very old Chinese legend that is a lesson not to judge by appearances. And it goes like this:

"Once upon a time there was a Chinese farmer who had an old horse with whom he worked his lands. One day the horse ran away and when the other farmers came to console him for his bad luck, the farmer replied: "Bad luck? Good luck? Who knows?" A week later the horse returned with a herd of wild horses and the neighbors came, this time, to congratulate him on his good luck. His response was: "Good luck? Bad luck? Who knows?" Later, when the farmer's son was trying to tame one of the wild horses, he fell and broke his leg. They all thought that this was very bad luck, except for the farmer, whose reaction was the same: "Bad luck? Good luck? Who knows?" One week later, the army passed through the village recruiting all the youths in conditions of being trained to go to war. Was this now good luck? Bad luck? Who knows?"

On the other hand, we are inclined to think that our values, our ethics, our morals, our sexual orientation and our sense of duty are all that is and should be. Be careful! Not make the mistake of judging others. Jesus warns us in Matthew 7:1-2: **"Judge not, that you be not judged. For with what judgment ye judge, ye shall be judged; and with what measure ye mete, it shall be measured to you again."** Once again you would set in motion the law of cause and effect or karma, immediately separating you from God.

In our spiritual growth it is very important *to develop an awareness of not judging by appearances*. The illusory appearances of this world, both good and bad, change by touching that spiritual consciousness. As we develop our faculty of *spiritual discernment*, the *"invisible becomes visible."* We manage, in this way, to eliminate our fear, our hatred or our love for appearances. So, there is nothing to fear nor anything to rejoice in because what you're seeing with your human eyes is not a spiritual creation of God but an optical illusion of our senses: sometimes good and sometimes bad, sometimes poor and sometimes rich, sometimes healthy and sometimes sick, sometimes "alive" and sometimes "dead". *But none of that is real in "My Kingdom", the place where I live, I move and I have my being.*

To develop that spiritual awareness it is necessary that you start acting like you have it. As long as you do the effort to see this material world of appearances without making judgments, neither good nor bad, you will be advancing in your spiritual development; even if at this moment you don't see it like that with your human eyes. Just trying to see God's creation as God sees it is one more step you are taking toward higher consciousness. *Now is the time to begin to consciously accept the Truth.* Your mind already knows how to intellectually differentiate between what is fictional and what is real; force it to accept the real and ignore the fictitious. *You can now control your mind. Do it!*

4.4 CONTROL YOUR MIND AND YOUR THOUGHTS

In the sacred scriptures of the Hindus, The Bhagavad Gita, which together with the Bible is one of the most translated books in the world, the following is read in Chapter six, Text 6:

"For him who has conquered the mind, the mind is the best of friends; but for one who has failed to do so, his mind will remain the greatest enemy."

And continues to say: *"For one who has conquered the mind, the Supersoul is already reached, for he has attained tranquility. To such man happiness and distress, heat and cold, honor and dishonor are all the same. As long as one's mind remains an unconquered enemy, one has to serve the dictations of lust, anger, avarice, illusion, etc., and thus his life and its mission are spoiled."*

The Master Jesus tells us in Matthew 15:11: **"Not that which goes into the mouth defileth a man; but that which comes out of the mouth, this defileth a man."** And later on he expands on this concept, by pointing out that what comes out of the mouth comes from the heart, which is where the bad thoughts come from: murder, adultery, immorality, sexual assault, thefts, false testimonies and slander. The heart is your human or mental consciousness which is where your thoughts and your emotions come from.

Now that you are aware of the importance of your mind and your thoughts, *you must become a guardian of your thoughts.* That is not an easy task, because it is estimated that a person has an average of sixty thousand thoughts a day. However, a practical way to control your thoughts is *to observe your emotions*. It is impossible to feel bad and at the same time to have positive thoughts. When you feel bad, you are on a negative frequency that attracts more bad things to you. It is like when you turn on the television or radio and choose a channel to receive certain programming that it gets you down.

A few weeks after the terrorist act of September 11, 2001 in New York, a private plane crashed into a building in Manhattan, terrorizing residents and the entire nation, thinking that it was another terrorist act. Then it was clarified that the cause had been a mechanical failure. There is a popular expression that clearly reflects that situation, which says: *"Welcome wrong, if you come alone."* Undoubtedly, *the similar attracts the similar*.

If you fear something, sooner or later, you are going to experience it! Refuse to accept negative thoughts! Be very careful when feeling depressed, distressed, or pessimistic, and immediately replace those feelings. Take control of your mind! Change the channel! Think of the omnipresence, omnipotence and omniscience of God, what is real. Spiritualize your thoughts, meditating and "practicing the presence of God."

Mind in its unenlightened state, which is the human mind, is void of truth, full of material beliefs, theories, opinions, doctrines and creeds that can only manifest their own state of chaos. What we call sin, disease, scarcity, pain, fear and anguish are only the absence of truth, the absence of God. *It is atheism!* No person is totally free from thoughts distressing, either for themself or for their loved ones, but in that moment those negative thoughts immediately separate you from God and his protection. Be very careful because, in addition, you are exerting a very negative influence on the people who are on the same frequency and do not know how to protect themselves. I repeat to you: *Refuse to accept negative thoughts!*

On the other hand, a mind, your mind or mine, filled with the truth is a blessing for you and the people around you. It is love, it is harmony, it is an influence for good and can even bring about healing. A mind imbued with truth opens consciousness. And a Spiritual Consciousness is not reached by physical power or mental power.

In the mystical literature of the East, we find a tale, written about 500 years B.C., illustrating the illusory nature of evil or error. It says so:

"It can easily happen that a man who is bathing, steps on a wet rope and mistakes it for a snake. The panic dominates and trembles with fear, anticipating in his thoughts the agony and death caused by the bite of a poisonous viper. How great is the relief of that man when he recognizes that it is not a snake but a rope! The cause of his fear was due to his mistake, his ignorance, to his illusion. Recognizing that it was a simple rope, he recovered his tranquility, his joy and his happiness. That's the same mental state of the one who recognizes that there is no evil and that the cause of all their problems, their desires and their vanities is a mirage, a shadow, a dream."

4.5 LEVELS OF A SINGLE CONSCIOUSNESS

In the beginning there was only one state of consciousness, the Spiritual. That is the first chapter of Genesis, where man is created in the image and likeness of God. At that time, the human being had fully developed his *spiritual sense,* and therefore was pure of thought and conscience. It was a *spiritual being* that lived exclusively of his inner life. He was not aware of good nor of evil, and his life was expressed externally in a harmonious way. When he felt the apparent need for something, everything he needed to do was close his eyes, go inside and let it manifest externally what he needed. That is the level of consciousness at which Jesus is referring to when he says to his disciples: **"Whatever things you desire, when you pray, believe that you receive them, and you shall have them"** (Mark 11:24). The Bible refers to that spiritual being symbolically like Adam and Eve, who lived a spiritual life without problems until they were expelled from the Garden of Eden.

From the so-called "fall of man", the human being, by an act of his own conscience, separates himself from the God-Conscience, which is the purest stage of consciousness, and is fundamentally divided in *two great stages of consciousness: mental and spiritual,* and in those two stages of consciousness there are so many levels of consciousness as there are people. In the entire history of mankind there have been very few people who have reached a Spiritual Consciousness.

Talking in terms of vibrational frequencies, *Spiritual Consciousness* is the highest level of vibrational frequency that a person can operate and is only reached by the mystics. You reduce the number of vibratory frequencies and find the stage highest of Mental Consciousness, which is *Cosmic Consciousness or Cosmic Mind*, which is the infinite source of all knowledge of this world: art, music, literature, science, inventions and discoveries. A person can be in tune with Cosmic Consciousness and not have an iota of Spiritual Consciousness and vice versa. If you reduce the number of vibratory frequencies a little more and we find the stage of *intuition*, which is the ability to understand something without the intervention of reason, intellect, the mind; it comes to us from the Spiritual Consciousness or God. It should not be confused with *instinct*, which is behavior from our karma, on impulse, that comes to us from past experiences in other lives, from the *subconscious mind*. For example, fear of heights that in a past life caused us death. That corresponds at that level of vibrations which is the *intellect*, that commonly known as the *mind*. Below the intellect we have the lowest vibration of mental consciousness, which is expressed as *matter*. *Matter is the name given to the mind when takes shape.*

Plato said that inspiration comes to people through poetry, but in reality inspiration or creativity comes to the individual when it connects with Cosmic Consciousness, which is the infinite source of all scientific and artistic knowledge. Once the idea is in the consciousness of the individual, then it is very easy for him to make it visible through his mind. Mozart (1756-1791) wrote in his letters: *"I heard it faster than I could write it"* and Beethoven (1770-1827), referring to one of his symphonies, said: *"It did not come from me, but through me."* The chief engineer who built the Golden Gate Bridge in San Francisco, one of the most important engineering achievements of the twentieth century, was asked how he had done it and his answer was: "Praying!" meaning by "praying" to give an attentive ear to God. So that, *the infinite library of the universe is in your own consciousness!*

Let's take another example: the invention of the wheel, which is one of the most important inventions of our civilization. Let's go back mentally to Antiquity and try to imagine the world without the wheel. Let us ask ourselves where did the wheel come from? Undoubtedly that of the mind of man, which is the door of entry and exit of our consciousness. The man goes into his conscience and connects with that Cosmic intelligence, infinite, eternal, omnipresent, omnipotent and omniscient. Once the idea of the wheel is in the conscience of the individual, then it is very easy for him to make the wheel visible through his mind. That same principle applies to radio, television, aviation, etc., and you will see that for a man to be creative, he has to receive inspiration from something that goes beyond his education. The person, first, has to receive all these things in his conscience and then you will be in a position to take the next step to externalize it through his mind.

4.6 MENTAL AWARENESS AND THE SUBCONSCIOUS

Through countless generations of the human race, man has lived in the state of mental consciousness and all that has been known is a material sense of the world, a mental world, where "thoughts are things" and "belief is biology." In this material world, the human being is the one who rules through physical or mental means creating a true chaos, where the strongest has always dominated and exploited the weakest. The bullets were imposed over the bows and arrows, then the cannons over the bullets, and now the bombs on the cannons. The human being has always used one power to defeat another power.

To better understand that concept of the *mental consciousness* of human being, let's take the following example from Hindu mysticism:

*"Imagine an infinite line in the middle of the darkness; the line we cannot see, but in that line there is a luminous point that moves along. As it moves it illuminates different parts in succession and everything that is left back turns into darkness. Our **mental consciousness** is like that luminous point, while past experiences come to constitute our **subconscious**. We are not aware of their presence, but unconsciously they are influencing our body and our mind."*

The **conscious mind** is just the tip of the iceberg and the millions of thoughts and actions from our past lives constitute our **subconscious mind**. Many of our current actions, whether good or bad, have their origin in the subconscious and are not under our control. By not being aware of our subconscious, it exerts a greater influence on our actions because we act on impulse, reflexively, involuntarily, without thinking nor measuring the consequences. We are good or bad despite ourselves. The bad actions of the human being are caused by the innumerable thoughts and actions that were conscious in the past but are now petrified in the subconscious, forgotten, invisible to our conscious, but that can suddenly manifest themselves with force. But just like bad actions can be located in the subconscious, good deeds can too. It is what Hindu mysticism calls the *law of balance*. It is really a tremendous psychological problem that we face daily.

The subconscious mind cannot differentiate between good and evil because its role is not to judge our thoughts and/or actions, but act. It just impulsively acts as a consequence of the stimuli it receives. This became obvious with the first experiments that were done using *subliminal perception*. In experiments carried out in the cinema, people were induced to get up from their seats and go to the phone. A majority of people obeyed the 'go to the phone' command, which was quickly thrown to the screen so they couldn't see it nor hear it consciously, only to find that they did not have no one to call. The idea that the behavior of a person can be influenced by external stimuli without the person having conscious knowledge caused a lot of controversy in the sixties. There was a very strong reaction from the public against companies that offered to massively improve sales of their customers' products by offering to post *subliminal messages* in theaters and in commercials. Consumers refused to be manipulated and the storm of protests led to the suspension of subliminal messages in the United States and in the most western countries.

Another example that shows how our subconscious operates is this: do you remember the first day you were at the wheel of a car? The amount of simultaneous things you had to do in your conscious mind was overwhelming: keep your eyes on the street and, at the same time, look in the rearview mirror and the sides, pay attention to the speedometer and other instruments, use your two feet in sync for the three pedals (something typical of the synchronous vehicles of the past), be aware of other vehicles, pedestrians, etc. It took you a while before all these actions were "programmed" in your mind. Today, years later, you get into your car, turn it on without thinking about the driving mechanics, while you consciously review mentally your shopping list or talk on the phone. Furthermore, sometimes we are so engrossed in our thoughts that we do not pay attention to our driving for minutes, yet we remain on our side of the road and respect the traffic signs. If we were not aware of driving the vehicle during that time, who was driving? *The subconscious mind!* The subconscious mind takes over in the moment when your conscious mind is not paying attention. However, the conscious mind can intervene at any moment and stop the behavior of the subconscious mind and create a new response.

Another characteristic of the subconscious mind is that it never lies. The lie detector is based precisely on that property of the subconscious. A person can consciously lie but the involuntary reactions of your body, controlled by the subconscious mind, give them away. Another classic example showing that the actions of the subconscious are by nature thoughtless and not controlled by reason or thought is the experiment of Russian scientist Ivan Pavlov (1849-1936), who conditioned his dogs to salivate at the sound of the bell.

4.7 THE UNIVERSAL HYPNOTISM

Universal hypnotism, which are the *universal beliefs of being human*, full of spiritual ignorance and limitations, is so invisible to the conscious mind like flashes thrown at the screen in the subliminal experiment and our subconscious mind is like a powerful antenna that collects all those universal beliefs of good and evil that separate us from God and are in the air constantly, keeping the human being in a hypnotic state.

Dr. Bruce Lipton (Professor of Cell Biology at the School of Medicine from the University of Wisconsin, and later in Stanford University School of Medicine), author of the book "The Biology of Belief" published in 2005, informs us that scientists have estimated that the *subconscious mind*, through sensory organs (sight, touch, hearing, smell and taste), can process twenty million stimuli per second, while the *conscious mind* reaches only a maximum of forty stimuli per second. That is to say, that *the subconscious mind can process in a second 500,000 times more than the conscious mind is capable of making*. The difference is astonishingly great and of extraordinary consequences on human behavior.

People, ignorant of what the subconscious is recording, are easy victims of the world's beliefs. There is an *unconscious collective*, of which the psychiatrist Carl Jung (1875-1961) speaks, which is the set of human experiences and beliefs that are transmitted from generation to generation, in a very difficult vicious cycle to break. Those false universal beliefs come to us through human thoughts, radio, television, newspapers; in short, they are the product of the general restlessness of the *conditioned mental consciousness* of the human being that is permanently in the air, 24 hours a day, as electromagnetic waves that act hypnotically on us, constituting what the mystics call *universal hypnotism*. Those universal beliefs of the general public are very difficult to eradicate from the individual conscience, but they only have power because the human mind accepts them.

When Jesus tells us in John 16:33, **"I have overcome the world"**, he's referring to that world constituted by universal beliefs which has no real existence. The *conditioned human mind* is an obstacle for the human being to realize the Truth, since the Truth received in conscience destroys the things that the human being has learned to love: personal splendor and glory, personal power, personal achievement or personal wealth. *The human mind is focused on glorifying herself individually.* It has nothing to do with the education of the person or with their religion but with the *universal hypnotism*, which is the factory of this human world.

The reality is that *we live under a hypnotic state sustained by the tyranny of our senses and by the universal hypnotism that it is broadcasting 24 hours a day*. We suffer a kind of collective schizophrenia and we live in a world of our own that has no correspondence with reality and in which, I repeat, *God does not participate and does not even know what is happening in that mental world of dreams and nightmares*. That is why the human experience is known as the "Adam's dream."

Now, having that you are aware of the duality of the human mind and the spiritual truths mentioned in this book, you are in a position to accept or reject in your conscience those universal beliefs full of lies and superstitions that your subconscious picks up from the environment. *Now you are able to recognize them! "Evil" only has power when we fail to recognize it.*

Moreover, from the moment of conception in the womb, our individual consciousness, through the subconscious, begins to receive conditions that are accentuated with the experience of birth and with everything our parents and relatives think. The fears, hopes and beliefs that they have in their minds, as well as the demonstrations of love or lack of love that they express, are transferred to the subconscious mind of the baby in formation. Countless investigations reveal that, from the moment of conception, the experience in the womb is decisive for the development of the brain.

Likewise, it is estimated that in the first six years of life the human brain operates at the lowest frequencies, delta and theta, which are the most programmable. During those years, the child absorbs an incredible volume of information into his subconscious coming from their parents and their environment. Information that is essential to adapt and succeed in their environment, and over time, he makes it his own as if they were absolute truths. As we are growing we are less susceptible to that external programming but, at the end of our adolescence, the effect of that whole set of experiences and influences is so powerful that our character, our belief system, feelings and emotions, our potential and even our biology are governed by that conditioning for the rest of our lives until we learn, once adults, to reprogram them in our conscience, if we have the will to do so.

All those sets of experiences and conditioning make your life a *unique life* different from mine and from all the others. In the words of Shakespeare (1564-1616*)*, *'The whole world is a stage, and all the men and women merely actors"* (As You Like It, Act II, Scene 7). You are playing a unique role, not only in the scene of this human life that you're living now but throughout all eternity. *You have always been and will continue to be an important and unique being in the universe for eternity!*

Now, knowing that what *we have in our conscience then passes to the subconscious*, we have the solution: *engrave spiritual truths on our consciousness so that they free us from those old beliefs in our subconscious.* To do this, we use the mind, which is the gateway to consciousness, to educate the mind through spiritual readings. It is, as the mystic Joel Goldsmith says, *"educate the mind through the mind itself."* That is a conscious act of our sole responsibility, since no one can do it for us.

4.8 EVIL IS NOT PERSONALIZED

A very important first step in our spiritual development is knowing the nature of evil or error. The nature of evil or error can be summed up in words such as "human mind", "carnal mind", "appearances", "temptation" "Satan", "demon", "sin," "devil," "antichrist," "ignorance," or "hypnotism." They are all synonyms.

It can be illustrated as follows: suppose there is a plant in the room where you are sitting with some friends and someone hypnotizes you and makes you believe that the branches of the plant next to you are snakes. Your reaction of fear and rejection will surprise your colleagues who are not hypnotized. But it doesn't matter what they tell you or what you do with those non-existent snakes, you will not be able to free yourself from them while staying hypnotized. The only way to get rid of them is to dehypnotize you. However, the last person to know that he is hypnotized is the person himself.

In the same way, it is possible to hypnotize you by making you believe that you are a human being separate and distinct from God. In the instant in which you accept in your mind that there is a God and something else, you are hypnotized. Every birth, every death, every limitation, every temptation that comes to us is the effect of that *universal belief* that only has power because the human mind accepts it, consciously or unconsciously. And since *there is only one Mind*, that is why we all see the same movie of human life. *Hypnotism creates absolutely nothing, except the temptation to believe that there is a condition or power other than God.*

Now, all sin that you see in the world is due exclusively to man's ignorance about his true spiritual identity. All the miseries and unhappiness of this world stem from the fact that for thousands of years we have accepted the hypnotic suggestion that we are human beings separate and distinct from God. All the selfish behavior of the human being is derived from accepting that great lie, and, consequently, we cling to the first law of the natural man, which is the law of survival. And that forces us all humans, in our spiritual ignorance, to break with Jesus's second command to **"love your neighbor as yourself"**, and the result is lies, deceptions, betrayals, wars, sickness and death.

Thus, evil, in whatever form or condition it presents itself, *it is absolutely impersonal*. The truth is that God constitutes the individual being and his nature is totally pure. Evil is not part of the spiritual identity of the human being nor can it become part of any man or woman. It can be removed by any enlightened person who makes it real in his conscience that this man or woman is God personified, and in his presence hypnotism dissolves.

Always remember that there is no person or condition to change. In the instant that you, conscious or unconsciously, try to change or improve a disease or a condition, you are *hypnotized*. Jesus showed us many times that we don't have to deal with the conditions that people present us with, but with *hypnotism. Hypnotism is the substance of cancer, Alzheimer's, immorality, poverty and unemployment!* There is only one enemy to defeat and only one demonstration must be made, and that is *the realization of the omnipresence of God.*

4.9 SPIRITUAL HEALING

The miracles of Jesus, which are mentioned in the gospels, are evidence that all human imperfections are nothing more than illusions or mirages, products of the *hypnotized mind* of the human being. To the invalid who had been paralyzed for thirty-eight years, Jesus said, **"Rise, take up thy bed, and walk"** (John 5:8); it is as if he had said: *"wake up from the hypnotism in which you find yourself."* To the man with a paralyzed hand, he said only: **"Stretch forth thine hand"** (Mathew 12:13). To the leper, he simply said: **"Be thou clean"** (Matthew 8:3). To Lazarus, who had been dead for four days and already started to decompose, he said to him: **"Lazarus, come forth"** (Juan 11:43). It's as if he had said: *"Death has no power, it is only an illusion."* He says to the stormy sea: **"Peace, be still"** (Marcos 4:39), as if to say: *"You are one more illusion, the only power is God."*

Moses and many other prophets performed spiritual healings long before Christianity existed. Also, five hundred years before Jesus there was an extraordinary ministry of spiritual healing throughout India carried out by the disciples of Gautama the Buddha. None of them applied any special or magical treatment.

Who then performs the miracles? It is not God. God has nothing to do with the material world. The light that radiates the Spiritual Consciousness of the enlightened person dispels all errors, all illusions, in the same way as darkness disappears when light comes. *Enlightenment, the power of Spiritual Discernment or Spiritual Consciousness or Christ Consciousness of the individual (all are synonyms), is what creates healing.*

To the extent that our consciousness is enlightened, that is, to the extent that we develop a Christ Consciousness, everyone who enters the radio of that Spiritual Consciousness is blessed. The people that have greater spiritual receptivity receive the greatest benefit.

For example, suppose you have a cold or cancer and you request the spiritual help of a person of enlightened Consciousness who practices spiritual healings. That person has no power over a cold or cancer, and neither does God. No one has power over those *conditions*, in the same way that they have no power over 2 x 2 = 5. We all know that 2 x 2 = 4 without using any power. Simply by knowing the Truth, the Truth sets you free of misconceptions. The spiritual practitioner knows the Truth that God did not create the cold or cancer or any other ailment and therefore there is no spiritual law to sustain them and consequently they have no real existence. Like Jesus, who did not apply any special treatment, the light that radiates the spiritual consciousness of the practitioner dissolves the error simply by knowing the Truth. **"You shall know the truth and the truth shall make you free"** (John 8:32).

There is a principle of spiritual healing that says: "*If it takes place in time and space, do not accept it at face value but search deep within your consciousness.*" Suppose you have an accident and every day you have a physical pain that you accept as "real." By recreating in your mind that problem over and over, what you do is reaffirm it. But if instead you say: "*Yes it took place in time and space therefore it is an illusion, a dream, a movie in my mind. It never happened because God is omnipresent and fills all spaces. God is the substance of each of my cells and organs of my body.*" If you repeat that several times a day for several weeks or months there will come a time when you make it real in your consciousness and from that moment all pain will disappear forever. This I tell you from my own experience. You have the ability to choose every day if you are going to live in omnipotent, omnipresent and omniscient consciousness, or if you are going to live in mental consciousness accepting appearances at face value. You choose every day if you are going to serve God or universal hypnotism and perpetuate the problem.

Personally, I can give testimonies of spiritual healings that I have received applying these spiritual principles. I witness that these healings are permanent in nature, as opposed to mental healings that are temporary while the hypnotic suggestion lasts. And if I could do it, and I am a person like you in search of his spiritual identity, you can do it too. It is a matter of daily practice, patience and perseverance of spiritual principles. *We started practicing those principles intellectually, day after day, week after week, month after month, until by repetition we manage to make it part of our consciousness realizing the Truth.*

4.10 DETACHMENT FROM THE THINGS OF THIS WORLD

The human being, by accepting in his conscience the "knowledge of the good and evil", has created a *mental world* and from then on his world was divided into good things and bad things in equal proportion. Of course that balance between good and bad is affected by the karmic bank that each person brings from previous lives.

As in the parable of the prodigal son, the human being enjoys the pleasures that worldly life offers him, but you can be sure that if he is enjoying the good things today, he will have to accept the bad things of tomorrow that will come to him in this or in the next life.

The spiritual masters of India compare the mind of the human being with the "crazy mind" of the monkey, and give us the following example:

"In India, to capture monkeys, they fill containers with grain, these containers have a very narrow neck that they place anchored in the ground as a hook. When the monkey comes for the grain, he puts his hand through the narrow neck of the container and grabs the grain by making a fist. When closing the fist he cannot get his hand out and is caught. Due to his greed, the monkey does not loosen his hand and, for a handful of grains, he loses his freedom and ends up dancing from door to door."

In the same way, the human being, by ignoring the true and eternal world by the desire to acquire and enjoy transitory things without any permanent value, ends up under the influence of the law of cause and effect or karma. We are haunted by a sense of the material so strong that it is hypnotizing. In the world exists an intense desire to acquire material things in order to increase our happiness, but after a certain time we realize that money doesn't buy happiness. It is what in psychology is called the "hedonic treadmill," which says that an increase in material wealth does not mean a long-term increase in the level of happiness of a person. Many people find themselves on that hedonic treadmill to find out that over time they return to their previous level of happiness after adjusting to the circumstances. All that eagerness to acquire things strengthens our hypnotism, moving us further away from God. Let's remember what the Bible tells us in Ecclesiastes 1:2-3: **"Vanity of vanities; all is vanity. What profit hath a man of all his labor which he taketh under the sun?"**

The human being achieves his sense of security and well-being only when he has acquired material goods, such as money in the bank, a good business or job, property or investments, even when he knows very well that these are temporary possessions, not permanent. However, the loss of those temporary possessions and/or sentimental losses leaves the human being without hope in the world and there are those who come in despair, to commit a greater sin which is suicide. The fear of losing his possessions and everything that entails: power, influences, relationships, well-being, prestige, etc., coupled with the struggle to obtain them are the cause of all the evils in the world. *Human beings do not realize that if you do not have God inside of you, you have nothing.*

Hindu mysticism tells us that the cause of all human miseries is *"the attachment to the things of this world."* There's a Buddhist saying that says, *"**The mind of the Buddha is the same in pleasure and pain.**"* It is true that for an enlightened mind both pleasure and pain are just an illusion. Detachment from the things of this world is the spiritual form.

We avoid feeling miserable when we have the power of detachment. The ideal is to be able to stick with all your strength and energies to the things that are worthwhile in this life but keep, with the same strength and energy, the power of detachment when you must do it. All human relationships, including parents, husbands, wives and children, are given to us in this life to realize, fulfill or satisfy this parenthesis of our existence. Jesus tells us in the name of God: **"He that loveth father or mother more than me is not worthy of me; and he that loveth son or daughter more than me is not worthy of me"** (Matthew 10:37).

For the mystics, to know God aright is to love God above all else. For them, God is the only real thing that exists who has to be loved and venerated every day and every moment of the day, not just for an hour on Sundays. God is the life of the universe expressed in infinite spiritual forms, the love of the universe, the Spirit omnipresent, omnipotent and omniscient that created, maintains and sustains the universe. What's more, *He is our true Father-Mother who has given us a happy and harmonious life for eternity.*

A person who has reached even a small level of spiritual consciousness can enjoy the things of this world, but never be tied to them. He would never be willing to cheat, lie or steal for them but enjoy them if they come to his experience in a normal and harmonious way, without loss or harm to others. Those people who achieve to some degree a *conscious realization of God* are those who have spiritual riches that neither time nor circumstances can affect. The only wish that serious students are allowed in their spiritual path is the desire to *experience God*. Any other desire should be gradually replaced by the desire *to know God aright*.

4.11 GOD IS OUR PROVIDER

One of the greatest concerns of human beings is their finances, that is even above their own health. Those who have a lot of money wake up thinking that they can lose it all or only a part of it, and those who have little or nothing wonder every day how they will fulfill their immediate commitments or those of their family.

According to an article in the *British Journal of Psychiatry*, the financial crisis from 2008 to 2010 caused at least 10,000 additional suicides in the United States, Canada and Europe. The Research found suicide rates skyrocketed drastically between 2008 and 2010, when millions of people lost their jobs and their homes. They also found that men are more likely to kill themselves, for cultural reasons that pressure you to be the breadwinner.

I have personally knew people who chose to kill themselves in difficult economic situations. All these pitiful and painful situations are the consequence of accepting an existence separate and distinct from God. These suggestions are so universal that they constitute the so-called *universal hypnotism*, and the only way to get rid of them is to live on a higher plane of consciousness. We must train ourselves mentally so that nothing that exists in the world of effects has any power over us. *We can no longer accept illusion, suggestion and hypnotism as reality.*

The statement that **"For the love of money is the root of all evil"** (I Timothy 6:10) is often misunderstood. There is nothing sinful about money, but putting your faith and your security in money is wrong. Money can never be our provider, and neither can our work, our investments or our properties. *God is our provider! God Himself is abundance!* If you have a billion dollars and you don't have God, you have nothing. Always keep that in mind, and by applying the spiritual principles you will always have abundance. Asceticism, a doctrine based on an austere lifestyle to achieve spiritual perfection is not the way to follow. That has never solved anyone's problem.

From a spiritual point of view, *abundance is God's law.* We can appreciate it in nature. If we look, for example, an orange tree or any other, we will find hundreds of fruits in each tree, and each fruit contains a large number of seeds, each of them capable of becoming a tree with hundreds of more fruits. Have you ever been into a jungle? You will find that there are not just many trees but too many trees. In John 6:1-15 Jesus multiplied the loaves of bread and fish to satisfy five thousand people and there were twelve baskets of fragments of the barley loaves left over. *Abundance is the Law of God!* In a world ruled by God there is no scarcity.

The secret of abundance is in Luke 12:22-31. There, Jesus addressing his disciples told them: **"Take no thought for your life, what ye shall eat; neither for the body, what ye shall put on. The life is more than meat, and the body is more than raiment. Consider the ravens, for they neither sow nor reap, which neither have storehouse nor barn and God feedeth them; how much more are ye better than the fowls? And which of you by taking thought can add to his stature one cubit? If ye then be not able to do that thing which is least, why take ye thought for the rest? .... And seek not ye what ye shall eat or what ye shall drink, neither be ye of doubtful mind. For all these things do the nations of the world seek after, and your Father knoweth that ye have need of these things. But rather seek ye the kingdom of God, and all these things shall be added unto you."**

It is important to note that this is being told by Jesus to his disciples, that is, people with a higher level of consciousness than the common people. Jesus is teaching his disciples that one of the fundamental principles to demonstrating abundance is the principle of "no reaction" or "zero anxiety." *The "devil" or Universal hypnotism takes hold of you when it scares you.* Remember that when we have doubt, fear or anxiety we are being atheists; that is, we do not have God. How can you expect the infinite abundance of God to be manifested in you if you don't have God? Always keep in mind that **"In quietness and in confidence shall be your strength"** (Isaiah 30:15).

We cut off our supply source when we put our faith in social security or unemployment insurance or in any government or company out there for our livelihood, rather than looking for that source of supply within ourselves. *God is my abundance, God is my provider and the only God that I have is the one I find inside of me.* It doesn't make any sense praying to God for supplies because there is no God out there who gives them to you. *I am abundance. Abundance is an activity of the Spiritual Consciousness. I personify abundance because the Father and I are one.* The key is to release that abundance so that it can come back to you. **"Cast thy bread upon the waters, for thou shall find it after many days"** (Ecclesiastes 11:1). The *"throwing our bread into the waters"* is to give an outlet to our Christ Consciousness, which is the "active principle", the source of abundance, and its function is to manifest itself externally in some way.

The only thing that can be increased or multiplied is what we have in our "house", *in our conscience*. Let's remember the story of Elisha, who asks the widow: **"What do you have in your house?"** (II Kings 4:2). And she said, **"Your servant has nothing in the house, but a pot of oil."** Yet from that pot of oil abundance came out. We too must start with what we have in house. "House", in the mystical sense, means our state of *realized consciousness*. What do I have in my realized consciousness? How aware am I that God is my provider? I must have something to start and set the law of abundance in motion. Look for something, either within yourself, in knowledge or that belongs to you that you can give. That would be to *"cast your bread"* and would put in motion the spiritual law of abundance. Giving something that you have and that is important to you, it is an act of trust that the supply is infinite and comes from the invisible. *By giving, the invisible becomes visible.*

The spiritual law of abundance is like a hose that has to be open at both ends for the water to flow and we all benefit from the flow. **"Whoever has will be given more, and they will have an abundance. Whoever does not have, even what they have will be taken from** them" (Matthew 13:12). It sounds like a very cold and cruel statement but it is a spiritual law that should always be taken into consideration.

A major obstacle to your spiritual supply is maintaining belief that someone is indebted to you, even if that is true from the human point of view. Immediately free yourself from that idea that someone is in your debt. You don't have to tell the person, because paying the debt can be essential for their spiritual growth. In this matter of loan, Jesus tells us in Matthew 5:42: **"Give to the one who asks you, and do not turn away from the one who wants to borrow from you."** Now the question is: how much and under what circumstances? It is advisable to give what you can freely give without any ties.

There is something very important that needs to be taken into account and it is the following: **"For the earth is the Lord's, and everything in it"** (I Corinthians 10:26). We do not possess absolutely anything. Not a house, not a piece of clothing, not a penny. Everything has been loaned by the Grace of the Father, for our use. Being in knowledge of that spiritual reality is essential to demonstrate our abundance. All our abundance comes to us from God, even though it comes to us apparently through people, places or conditions. Our obligation is to be good stewards of the assets that God has entrusted us. Do not forget that life will ask us to account for the use that you make of the goods that the Lord lent us, who in turn tells us: **"Son, thou are ever with me, and all that I have is thine"** (Luke 15:31).

4.12 THE MIND AND ITS POWER

The Mind is the human faculty of the intellect; that is, to learn, understand and reason. Furthermore, it is the instrument through which the activity of Consciousness takes place. *It is the entrance and exit door of Consciousness. The secret of the mind is that it is only one.* Your mind, my mind and all other minds are fragments of that unique Mind, like small waves in the ocean as the yogis say.

At the level of Spiritual Consciousness, that one Mind is unconditioned. That means it has no good or bad qualities, there is no intelligent mind or ignorant mind, healthy mind or sick mind. In other words, *the unconditioned Mind is totally transparent* and thus allows the Spiritual

Consciousness or God to express itself with all clarity, creating infinite spiritual and perfect forms.

In the human world, *that one Mind is conditioned by the knowledge of good and evil accepted in the human consciousness.* And because that mind is the mind of the individual being, your mind, mine and everyone else's, the whole world receives the same impressions and impulses of that only *one conditioned Mind.* And so, we are tempted 24 hours a day not only by what the world calls sin but also by the pair of opposites: harmony and discord, poverty and abundance, sickness and health, birth and death, and all degrees in between.

In the spiritual world, the mind has no power, since it is unconditional and transparent. But in our human world *the mind is not only the instrument of intellectual fulfillment but it has all the power of the material world.* However, once you have reached a Spiritual Consciousness, the mind has no power over you.

In ancient times, knowing how to read and write were skills that not even kings dominated. The only way to get an education was to enter the so-called schools of wisdom and mysteries that existed thousands of years ago in India and Egypt, and later in Greece and in Rome. In those cultures, where the important thing was to achieve physical power and military conquests, only young people with marked religious or philosophical tendency entered these schools of religious orders or secret fraternities from an early age with the purpose of achieving enlightenment. The graduates of those schools of spiritual development constituted the so-called *white brotherhoods.* However, some of those schools deviated from their original purpose and founded what is known by the name of *black brotherhoods,* made up mainly of men who, discovering the power of the mind, used it for their own glorification and personal gain, influencing others.

Thus, two types of schools developed, one next to the other. Those that taught the power of the mind and the purely spiritual, revealing the development of a Spiritual Consciousness. It is very important for aspirants of spiritual development to know the difference between these two approaches: *the mental as opposed to spiritual.* Everything that exists on the mental and material plane of life corresponds to *mental consciousness* and can be used to do good or to do evil. In contrast, the

Spiritual Consciousness cannot be manipulated and only expresses itself in good things.

The power of the mind over plants has been documented extensively in scientific work carried out by Dr. Franklin Loehr, Presbyterian minister and scientist, who in 1959 published his experiments in a book entitled "The Power of Prayers on Plants", causing impact on both the scientific and religious community. Dr. Loehr demonstrated in controlled seed germination experiments the effect of *positive prayer*. In it, *love* was expressed to seeds, telling them that they were very loved and that they were held and maintained by God. These positive prayers accelerated the seed germination and produced vigorous plants. Other groups of plants received *negative sentences*, such as: "you are ugly and nobody wants you; you don't belong to this universe and you must die." These plants ended up wilting and died within days of being despised.

The power of the mind also works in people. One of the most cited scientific studies had been carried out between the years of 1982 and 1983 in the coronary care unit of the General Hospital of San Francisco with 393 patients. Those patients who received prayers, without them knowing, had fewer complications, recovered faster and among them there were fewer deaths than those who did not receive them.

But don't think that God has something to do with growth accelerated plants or with heart patients. God has nothing to do with that. **"For God does not show favoritism"** (Romans 2:11). Furthermore, God does not operate in the material world of the human being. *It is the mental energy released by those positive thoughts which positively affects the material world.*

Another example of mental power over people can be found in books that have been written on witchcraft and voodoo, which give testimony of people who have entered the field *purely mentally* for the purpose of controlling others. In Hawaii, for example, we find the good kahunas and the bad kahunas. The good kahunas are those who think well about you and allow you to prosper and even cure yourself of some disease, while the bad kahunas are those who with their bad thoughts can make you sick and can even kill you.

In all primitive societies we find healers or witches who apply their *mental power* on others. If you are at the human level of *mental consciousness* you can be one more victim of those strong minds, but once you've developed to some degree a *Spiritual Consciousness* you are left out from the reach of mental power.

As a person rises spiritually, the secrets of the mind are revealed without seeking them. It's like being on top of a mountain and looking down, getting a vision much wider than those found in the valley. Human beings who have attained a Spiritual Consciousness can see within the minds of those who lead a mental and material life. They are not reached by mental power, even though they know very well how the mind operates and how it can be manipulated, but they don't do it for ethical reasons.

On the mental level, great feats of magic can be performed that can even be confused with those that are of spiritual origin. The Bible, in Exodus 7 to Exodus 12 tells us the miraculous wonders imparted by God, which Moses had to perform before Pharaoh to bring the children of Israel out of Egypt. However, some of those wonders (such as transforming their rods into serpents, turn the waters of the Nile into blood and infest frogs all over the country) were mentally replicated by Egyptian magicians. Until finally when they could not continue repeating the miraculous deeds of Moses, the magi recognized before Pharaoh that in all that Moses did was the hand of God.

The great Hindu mystic Swami Vivekananda (1863-1902), in a lecture he gave in Los Angeles in 1900 on "The Powers of the Mind", recounts his experience with a man from India who could predict events and read minds. He says that, out of curiosity, he and five friends came to see this man in an act, and that to avoid mistakes they previously wrote the questions they were going to ask him. As soon as the man saw them arrive, he repeated their questions and answered them. Then this man wrote something in a paper which he then folded and asked Vivekananda to sign it on the back and put it in his pocket. He asked the others people to do the same. Then he said: "Now think of a word or sentence in the language you want." Vivekananda thought a long prayer in Sanskrit, a language he thought the others did not know. "Now, take the paper from your pocket," the mentalist told them. To the surprise of Vivekananda, the Sanskrit prayer was written there. Another of his friends had thought of an Arabic sentence taken from the Koran, which the man was less likely to know, and the friend found that phrase written on the paper. Another friend was a doctor who thought of a phrase from a medical book written in German; and the phrase was written on his paper.

On another occasion, in the city of Hyderabad, India, Vivekananda tells us about another person who could produce things that no one knew where they came from. This man was half naked, covering only his private parts with a strip of clothing. He sat on a corner and covered her body with a sheet. And he said: "Write the names of the fruits that you want." They wrote the names of exotic fruits that did not grow in India, such as grapes, oranges, bananas and others, and the clusters of said fruits began to come out from under this man's sheet, so many that if they would have weighed them, they would have doubled the weight of the man. Then the man asked them to eat the fruits, which some objected because they thought it was hypnotism. However, the man began to eat them and they all did the same. The man finished the act by producing a bouquet of perfect roses with dew on the petals, without any damaged rose.

Vivekananda tells us that there are hundreds of acts like these in different parts of India and that thousands of years ago such cases abounded, but with the increase in the population the psychic powers have been deteriorating. Hindus, being people with a very analytical mindset, have made a science of this and have found that there is nothing supernatural about it. That is not a rarity of nature for someone to be born with these powers since, although extraordinary, are natural and can be systematically studied, acquired and practiced by all, because they are governed by laws, like any other physical phenomenon. That science is called Raja-Yoga.

In America, the illusionist Criss Angel has caused sensation in Las Vegas with his mentalist prowess. Using the streets of the city and the hotel pools as a setting, he has led magic at a much higher level than the once famous Houdini and the more recently famous David Copperfield. Criss Angel lifted off the ground, counteracting the law of gravity, amidst astonished crowds; walks on waters, crossing the hotel pools where people are bathing; walk the walls of buildings perpendicularly, as if he were a fly; he walks through the air from the terrace from one building to another, as if he had supernatural powers. When a journalist compared him to Jesus Christ for the fact of walking on water, he was quick to clarify that his acts were not spiritual at all but hundred percent mental.

I have had my personal experience with the use of the mind to influence other people. When I started my studies in college I was drawn to articles or books on the power of the mind and read them with great interest, trying to put them into practice in my studies. For example, when I didn't have time to study all the subjects, I concentrated on the teacher transmitting my thoughts about the topics he should ask. Most of the time I was successful, but in my skeptical mind I did not know whether to attribute the good results to power of the mind or mere chance, so I never took the matter very seriously. Until one day it was time for me to put that knowledge into practice. That was the day that I graduated abroad and my mother gave me money with which I bought a used car with very few miles. When I called the Venezuelan Consulate General in Philadelphia to authorize me to enter my vehicle into the country, they informed me that the car, in order to be entered, had to have at least one year of being purchased. That was devastating to me; first, because it was the gift from my mother and represented all my capital; and second, because I could not forgive myself for having acted rashly without due information. So, I said to myself: "If you had the mental capacity to graduate from a reputed university, use that same mind to get out of this predicament you've gotten yourself into." Immediately, I called and asked the Department of Motor Vehicles for a copy of the title deed of my car as soon as possible, arguing that I had lost the original; and quickly I started to focus on the specific date the copy had to have to meet with the laws of my country. I spent a week in a motel in Philadelphia waiting for the arrival of that paper to be able to return to Venezuela and I spent all that week concentrating on the purchase date that the vehicle should have. I clearly remember, even though more than 50 years have passed, that the copy of the property title was blue, instead of the yellow color that was the original, and it had written across the entire length of the title in large letters in red: "Copy", and, to my amazement, it had exactly the date that I had been transmitting mentally. I couldn't believe it myself!

Nowadays, the internet abounds in the offers of courses that manipulate the human scene with the right thought. For example, if you want a home, all you have to do is hold the right thought, visualize it and so the house appears; if you don't have the right partner, a little right thought is enough to make the old partner moves away from you and a new one appears; if you have a health problem, you keep the right thought and the illness disappears. But even though these kinds of mental exercises can be effective, and often are, those who use this technique are still subject to the ups and downs of the mental world. The next day it is very possible that discords and disharmonies begin again. In addition, using our mind to create something or attract people is to remove the mind from its natural orbit as an instrument of consciousness, and we can attract something that is not the best for us.

All these mental manipulations and others, like moving objects at a distance or bending silverware with the mind, transfer of thoughts or telepathy, perceptions of the astral world through the 'Sixth sense', perception of events in the future or in the past (known as clairvoyance), etc., all belong to the stage of *Mental Consciousness* of the human being. They are part of the *Universal Mind*, where each mind is connected to all the other minds. It is what yogis call the '*continuity of mind*', where each mind is part of that universal Mind, as waves in the ocean, and in consideration of that continuity, we can transmit our thoughts and feelings to other beings, both on the physical plane as well as on the astral plane.

Now all those *psychic experiences*, even though they may have application in our human experience, are *mental* and can be used to do good or evil. Stay away from those invisible "people" that continue in the mental world and can hurt you. They have nothing to do with the spiritual world. The fact of dying does nothing spiritual to you. No mystical literature refers to these phenomena as a spiritual experience. That is why our interest should be focused exclusively on our *spiritual development*, which is what opens the gates of heaven for us. There is no time to lose.

4.13 A PERSONAL GOD THAT DOES NOT EXIST

The human being of all religions and races has created a personal "God" somewhere up there, made in his own image and likeness, a superman who knows good and evil that only exists in the fantasy mind of the people. Religious teachings are the greatest obstacle to your spiritual growth because they have anchored your faith in a non-existent "God" separate and distinct from you, difficult to get rid of because for centuries a false concept of God has been engraved in your subconscious and in your mind. *Everything has been a huge deception to humanity of what we are all suffering.*

For thousands of years, humanity has been praying and offering to that "God" created by man, to eliminate wars, epidemics, plagues, droughts, storms, diseases, poverty, injustices in the world, to no avail. That has been nothing more than a waste of time and energy, the result of spiritual ignorance and superstition that has prevailed in the human world. *The world has been deceived.* And people have lost their reincarnation by making them believe that if they are good religious people they will find God and live for eternity after their death. That is totally untrue.

That chaotic image of the material world we live in is the direct result of the *Mental Consciousness* of the human being, and to change that image you simply have to raise human consciousness to the level of spiritual consciousness, which automatically would bring a change in our external experience, because what is realized in consciousness is what is manifested externally. Even though the principle is simple, that change of consciousness is nothing easy to reach. In fact, it is extremely difficult, because it requires a total change in human values and our concept of reality. Remember what Jesus tells us in Matthew 7:14: **"But small is the gate and narrow the road that leads to life, and only few find it."** If at the individual level that change in consciousness that "leads to life" is extremely difficult, on the collective level it is nothing short of impossible. Only God can do it.

In this second creation, which is exclusively of man, God does not intervene at all. In the words of the French philosopher Voltaire (1694-1778), *"In the beginning God created man in His own image, and man has been trying to repay the favor ever since."* The stark truth is that God has never participated in human affairs, except in those cases where a person through his own spiritual development becomes a transparency through which God manifests himself externally. *God can only manifest in the human world through the enlightened consciousness of some individual being.* When this happens, God, indeed, makes Himself felt and the healing, the harmony and peace are the result.

What we know as sin, disease, scarcity, pain, fear and death are only the absence of God, as well as the darkness is only the absence of light. What's more, God can't see the inequities of human life in the same way as light can't see dark. This is not theoretical speculation, but a fact that has been proven countless times by the enlightened of all ages, through spiritual healings that we have mentioned above.

The apostle Paul warns us in I Corinthians 2:14 that **"But the natural man receive not the things of the spirit of God, for they are foolishness unto him"**; in the same way, we can say that God does not perceive the things of the natural man, which are all humans beings, because for Him human beings do not exist. The things of the human being known by mystics as the "Adam's dream", which are all vicissitudes of this earthly world, are not perceived by God. *Always remember this when you are tempted to bring your human problems to God.*

4.14 GOD DOES NOT PARTICIPATE IN HUMAN AFFAIRS

The fact that God does not participate in human affairs has tremendous implications from an international, national, social and individual point of view. The Old Testament, for example, is full of stories of people and nations that ask God to destroy their enemies. The first death in the Bible is the murder of Abel at the hands of his brother Cain because of his jealousy or envy of God's "preference" for Abel. From there, wars and murders are a constant in the history of mankind, where the belief that God is on either side plays a primordial role. We still hold the belief today that we can use God for our purposes.

From the social point of view, we can point out, for example, that the Catholic church, by opposing birth control for theological reasons and discarding all kinds of socioeconomic reasons, has affected and continues to negatively affect economic and social development of Latin America, whose population is eminently Catholic. In this way, the dogmatism of the Catholic Church has contributed enormously to the overwhelming growth of the marginal population, which has resulted in increased misery, ignorance and crime throughout Latin America, to the point that it is already uncontrollable. Even though Latin America is not a theocracy, which is the government in the hands of the clergy Muslim style, the Catholic influence in government decisions such as birth control is undeniable. It should be noted that populist parties have conveniently supported the uncontrolled growth of the marginal population, based on the premise that the greater the poverty, the greater the uptake of votes for their parties. The concern of populist leaders for the poor is rarely genuine. They generally use demagoguery with easy flattery and unfounded promises to get through to power and, once this is achieved, they use it for their own benefit.

Human nature does not change. When the sisters of Lazarus, Martha and Mary make a dinner for Jesus in gratitude for having resurrected her brother who had died, Mary took a pound of ointment of spikenard, of great value, and anointed the feet of Jesus. Judas Iscariot, one of the disciples (the one who was to deliver Jesus for thirty pieces of silver) said: **"Why was not this ointment sold for three hundred pence and given to the poor?"** And the Bible tells us: *"This he said, not out of love for the poor, but because he was a thief, and had the bag, and bare what was put in."* But Jesus said, **"Leave her alone, it was intended that she should save this perfume for the day of my burial. You will always have the poor among you, but you will not always have me"** (John 12: 7-8). And in Deuteronomy 15:11 it is said: **"There will always be poor people in the land."** The populists leaders fail to understand that the only true revolution is the change of consciousness of the individual, in particular, of themselves; and the best system of government is the democratic system with free, fair and universal elections.

Individually, many people think that bringing children to the world is under the control and guidance of God. They think that it is a blessing that God has given them, and consequently they do not nothing to avoid them. The truth is that this is not a divine decision, but a purely human decision in which God does not participate and of which He does not even know because His world is spiritual, eternal, where there are no births or deaths. There is no such thing as the creation of new babies. Babies are born, but they are not created, since they have existed as spiritual beings for millions of years and they are manifesting visibly at this level of consciousness. But God has not created anything or anyone today because everything that exists has been created from the very beginning. We repeat: **"All things were made by Him, and without Him was not anything made that was made"** (John 1: 3).

I must clarify that human beings give birth to human beings, while spiritual beings give birth to spiritual beings. Jesus confirms this to us in John 3:6, when he tells us: **"That which is born of the flesh is flesh, and what is born of the Spirit, is spirit."** It all depends on the combined stage or level of consciousness of the parents. Before you were born, your conscience was working to produce the seeds that were used to bring you into this world, while you chose those parents whose level of vibrations combined was the same as yours because you felt, at that moment, in harmony with them. On the other hand, we have said that God only manifests in this world through the enlightened consciousness of the people. If parents have a spiritual consciousness that is in constant gratitude to God for having given them the opportunity to be the instrument for another spiritual consciousness to manifest in this world, and express daily love to that seed that is formed by the Grace of God in the womb, then, that will be a very special baby. Hindu mystic Swami Vivekananda accounts that his father and mother were meditating and fasting for years before he was born.

On the other hand, in a lecture by Lorraine Sinkler (outstanding student of Joel Goldsmith and mystic in her own right) in which I participated in 1977, I remember they asked her opinion on *abortion*. Her answer was simply that *life is indestructible*. Evidently, *everything created by God is indestructible*. God cannot give life eternal and at the same time give death. That is a contradiction. If so, the concept of God would not be valid because God is eternal and universal life. Life is a spiritual activity and when you are in knowledge of that truth you will be able to understand that life is indestructible. There has never been a dead or diseased person, animal or plant because everything is spiritual and eternal. *Abortion is a very personal decision that should be guided by the conscience of each individual of what it is right or wrong under the circumstances of the moment. We are not allowed to judge, much less governments to legislate in this regard.*

It must not be forgotten that thoughts, words or human actions set in motion the law of cause and effect or karma, but at no time do they offend, please or exercise any influence on God. When we give thanks to God because He gives us a child, a good job, health, etc., it is not because God waits for our thanks and He would be mad if we don't. No. It is not for God that we should do it, but for ourselves. Just feeling grateful and loving God for all that we receive in life (good or bad, since we should not judge by appearances) generates a positive energy of thoughts that returns in some way to ourselves and benefits others in the process. **"Cast thy bread upon the waters, for thou shall find it after many days"** (Ecclesiastes 11: 1). In English there is a popular saying that expresses exactly the same thing: *"What goes around, comes around."*

4.15 THE THIRD AND FOURTH DIMENSION

When I speak of dimensions I am not referring to dimensions in geometry, space, time, physics or quantum physics. I am referring to dimensions of life in the three levels of Consciousness: physical, mental and spiritual, also called the three major Planes of Existence. As human beings we live in the *Third Dimension* that includes the *physical plane* and the *mental plane*. Our body is under physical law and our mind is under mental law, as I mentioned at the beginning of this chapter. In this Third Dimension we are trapped in two powers: the power of good and the power of evil, and we are subject to the Law of Cause and Effect or Karma. When you make your transition and leave this physical plane, you continue to live on the mental plane exclusively which is the Astral World and which the mystics consider another world of illusion, maya. And you will continue to be trapped in those two powers of good and evil, paying karma until you get off that "Wheel of Life" that is the repeated cycle of birth, life, death, life after death and rebirth, with all the suffering that it entails according to our karma. It goes on and on until, tires of so much pain, like the prodigal son, we have an spiritual awakening.

According to the occultism, as we mention earlier in the sub-chapter 3.9, the Astral World consists of seven planes that have seven sub-planes, and each of these sub-planes have their own seven subdivisions, and so on to the seventh degree of subdivision. But instead of planes rising one above the other in space, they are composed of vibration of energy. They are graded according to their respective degrees of *vibration of energy*, and they interpenetrate each other in the same point of space and yet not interfering with the others. There is an ancient aphorism that says: *"A plane of being is not a place, but a state of being."* The vibration of the lower planes, according to the occultists, are very unpleasant to souls who have them.

The Fourth Dimension, also called by the mystics the kingdom of God, is the Spiritual Plane. It is the only way to reach God. There is no other way. Karma no longer exists. This Fourth Dimension is not found after death, but it is *now and here*; is this Third Dimension seen with a much higher level of consciousness, with new eyes. The *"invisible, that is the eternal, becomes visible"* when the faculty of *spiritual discernment* awakens in us. And that faculty, also called *Spiritual Consciousness* or *Christ Consciousness*, is the faculty of being able to see what is not evident to the mind. And it is the one that expresses itself in harmony, abundance, health and life. That is why mystics live in "heaven" while on earth. *"They live in the world, but not of the world."*

For our physical senses and our mind, the ills that we confront in this life appear as real entities, very personal and painful. But for a *spiritual consciousness, also called fourth dimensional consciousness, Christ consciousness or Buddha-mind* (They are all synonymous) they are not realities, in the sense that they only exist as a product of the *universal hypnotism* of which we all humans are victims. We find beauty in people, things and circumstances that are not beautiful, just as we find ugly people, things and circumstances where there is nothing ugly. All because we react to the *universal beliefs* that are constantly being transmitted in the air like electromagnetic waves.

The earth seen with the eyes of the fourth dimension is heaven and the heaven seen with the eyes of the third dimension is the earth. As in heaven, so on earth. This is literally true. *Heaven is a stage or level of consciousness, not a locality. Heaven is everywhere because it is infinite.* It is not found "up there," as the religious say. The world is the temple of God. The world is not an illusion. The illusion is in our sense of the world. God never created an illusion. The outside world is always the same. Outside there is nothing different. God did create the world which to human sense is seen "**through a glass darkly**" (I Corinthians 13:12). Let's remember the famous poem by the Spanish Ramón de Campoamor (1817-1901), who says: *"And it is that in the traitorous world / nothing is Truth or lie / everything is according to the color / of the glass with which you look."* The difference is in the degree of spiritual awareness that the individual has developed. That determines the degree of heaven that we experience, while the lack of that spiritual awareness determines the degree of hell that we experience.

The destiny of each and every person is fulfilled when reaching the *Fourth Dimension*, where each act is motivated by divine, unconditional, impersonal and universal LOVE. In the third dimension each act is motivated by FEAR, a consequence of our human sense of survival. Until your consciousness is not enriched and expanded, your world cannot be enriched and expanded. For the mystics, *you are not in the world but the world is in you.* That coincides with a wise Spanish proverb that says: *"Every head is a world."*

4.16 QUANTUM PHYSICS AND MYSTICISM

Quantum physics, which studies the universe of subatomic particles, shows us that our physical body and the whole material universe that surrounds us are nothing more than a field of energy in constant transformation and exchange of circulating atoms freely throughout the cosmos, and that, moreover, *responds to our conscience.* Everything is malleable, nothing is solid. Quantum physics contradicts common sense: everything seems to be a contradiction. Nevertheless, quantum physics has been spectacularly successful in predicting physical phenomena, since without it an abundance of objects such as transistors, radios, televisions, computers, cell phones, microwaves, etc., would not be possible.

One of the pioneers of quantum physics, Werner Heisenberg (1901-1976), demonstrated that the subject or person (who in language physics is the observer) alters what is observed by the simple fact to observe it. That is, *observation affects the observed reality!* Heisenberg says that atoms are not things but tendencies. Therefore, instead of thinking about things, you have to think about possibilities. Quantum physics is the physics of possibilities. An electron or quantum can act as a wave or as a particle (this is called duality wave-particle) and can be in two places at the same time! And the only time it acts as a particle is when we are looking at it!

Later experiments have led some scientists to suggest that human *consciousness does affect matter.* In 1984, John Wheeler and Wojcieck Zurek, in their Quantum Theory and Measurement, indicated that observers are necessary to give existence to the material world. Isn't that what the mystics tell us about the creation of the second and third chapters of Genesis is the product of the mental consciousness of the human being?

Two eminent scientists of our time, David Bohn (1917- 1992, University of London physicist, Einstein protégé and one of the most respected in quantum physics) and Karl Pribran (1919- 2015, Professor Emeritus at Stanford University and author of Languages of the Brain, a Classic Textbook in Neuropsychology), arrived, independently and studying different fields of science, to the same conclusion: *the universe is a gigantic hologram, image with a three-dimensional optical effect, constructed by the human mind.*

Scientists previously thought that there was a direct correspondence between the image that our eyes see and the image represented in our brain. In other words, it was believed that when we looked at an object, the electrical activity in our cerebral cortex took the same shape as the object. Nowadays, thanks in large part to Dr. Pribran, neurology has shed new light by pointing out that what the brain offers us is an interpretation of the electromagnetic waves that surround us and that materialize into objects in the brain. Through the collective subconscious we transform those energy fields into a common "reality". Let's take the landscape we see around us as an example. Our conscious mind sees it as the "real" world but it is only an image or misleading representation of reality, like the mirage in the desert caused in the mind by the erroneous interpretation of the data provided by our senses. *What you perceive with your senses out there exists but does not exist in the way you think it exists. We are not seeing the world as it really is but as our mind interprets it.* Is this not what Gautama the Buddha revealed to us in the year 550 BC that this material world that we perceive with our senses is *maya or illusion*?

It has taken science more than two millennia to begin to accept what mystics had already experienced centuries ago that what we perceive as our "reality" is just a *mirage*. The unfortunate thing is that still, thousands of years after those extraordinary revelations of the mystics and corroborated today by quantum physics, the human race continues to be immersed in a sea of ignorance of reality, pitifully sustained and sponsored by different religious institutions. Consequently, humanity stubbornly remains in a state of denial.

4.17 RECAPITULATION

Now, as we recognize that the creation of the second and third chapters of Genesis is the human mind in action, we have the secret of their destruction: *to rise above the mind and thoughts. That is precisely the secret of a spiritual life.* The great mystic Isaiah confirms this to us by saying: **"For my thoughts are not your thoughts, neither are your ways my ways, says the Lord"**(Isaiah 55: 8). Our Thoughts are undoubtedly not the thoughts of God, but when we manage to silence the mind and replace the thoughts by silence, in the humble attitude of: **"Speak Lord, for your servant is listening"** (I Samuel 3:9), then **"God uttered His voice, the earth melted"** (Psalms 46: 6). The land referred to by the psalmist is not the land of God but the one to which Jesus refers when he says, **"My kingdom is not of this world"** (John 18:36). And "this world" is none other than the mental world of the human being made of sin, sickness, death, scarcity and limitation, which has no real existence because it is made of a false sense of separation from God.

We can no longer look at the material world around us in the same way as we did before. We are no longer the same. By regaining awareness of our true spiritual identity, we are no longer what we were. It is true that universal beliefs hammer our minds all the time: the universal beliefs of age, the universal beliefs of germs, the universal beliefs of finances, the universal beliefs of accidents, the universal beliefs of death, etc. But they come to our thoughts as beliefs or suggestions to be *accepted or rejected* by us. People who don't have knowledge of these things are innocent victims of the universal beliefs, but you are now aware of how they operate and that *gives you the power to accept or reject them. Now you can dehypnotize yourself!* Everything now depends on you. You already have intellectual knowledge, now it's your turn to put it into practice. You must already act with absolute confidence in that knowledge and begin to spiritualize your consciousness

One way to start spiritualizing your consciousness *is constantly practicing the presence of God.* Let's remind ourselves every moment that the omnipresence of the Grace of God is always present within us wherever we are, regardless of external appearances. Even when we do not feel the presence of God at that moment, we must consciously recognize the omnipresence of God in every act. I recommend you frequently read the last sub-chapter of the first chapter, entitled: "The secret of your Safety: Pray without ceasing". At first this is a mental exercise, but the seeds of Truth that we contemplate in our minds will grow in us, expanding our consciousness until we leave the state of Mental Consciousness and start the path to a Spiritual Consciousness.

Do not forget the importance of repetition. For example, to make the omnipresence of God part of your conscience, you must repeat it over and over from the moment you wake up in the morning until you go to bed at night and continue for fifty-two weeks a year until eventually that affirmation passes from your mind to your consciousness. But it is not repeating that statement as a mantra but contemplating its meaning day after day, week after week, month after month and year after year, until something says within you: "God is here." And *God is omnipresent, omnipotent and omniscient.* From that moment on, you can live your life with those three words and you have it all.

CHAPTER 5

The Duality Of Man

5.1 THE HUMAN BEING AND THE SPIRITUAL BEING

Let us remember what the Jesuit and mystic Pierre Teilhard de Chardin tells us about: *"We are not human beings who are having a spiritual experience. We are spiritual beings who are having a human experience."*

One of the paradoxes of the Bible, difficult to understand, is that seems that man is not one but two.

In the New Testament, Jesus tells us:

- **"I can of my own self do nothing"** (John 5:30);

- **"The Father that dwells in me, He does the works"** (John 14:10);

- **"If I testify about myself, my testimony is not true"** (John 5:31);

- **"If I glorify myself, my glory means nothing"** (John 8:54); y

- **"My God, my God, why have you forsaken me?"** (Mark 15:34).

And on the other hand, he tells us:

- **"I am the way, the truth and the life"** (John 14:6);

- **"I and my Father are one"** (John 10:30)

-**"He that has seen me has seen the Father"** (John 14:9)

-**"The Father is in me, and I in Him"** (John 10:38)

-**"I am the resurrection, and the life"** (John 11:25) (notice that he does not say; "I am going to be resurrected" but "I am the resurrection" which means: I am the power itself)

Master Jesus sometimes refers to himself as a human being and sometimes as the "Son of God", that is, he is speaking to us from two different points of view. When he speaks to us as a human being, he is speaking to us from the point of view of Jesus, a Jewish rabbi; and when he speaks to us as the "Son of God," he is speaking to us as the Christ, which is the Christian term to identify the spirit of God in man. So by taking into account those two different points of view, this paradox of the duality of man is resolved. Of course, theologians do not share this opinion because they live in an exclusively *mental world* that prevents them to *experience God*.

In reality, there is no such duality. The human being is a "walking dead" that does not exist in the eyes of God. We are spiritual beings created in the image and likeness of God. Remember that **"All things were made by Him and without Him was not anything made that was made"** (John 1:3). And also remember that **"God is Spirit"** (John 4:24) and **"that which is born of the Spirit is spirit"** (John 3:6). Finally remember that the nature of *God is infinite* because it is *omnipresent*, consequently, *everything is spirit*.

In the course of human history, some people began to perceive that there is a part of the man or the woman that it is divine, sacred, in contrast to the other part that is human. They discovered that there is a light within each person, a presence, a power: God.

The first information we have that this light appeared as a person he was in India, about 3000 years BC, under the name of Krishna, which means "Light" or "the Enlightened One". Krishna was the light that manifested for the first time to the world through the consciousness of a human being. Years later, it happened with Gautama the Buddha, who it also means "Light" or "the Enlightened One" and it is the same

Spiritual Consciousness that was expressed through Krishna. About 500 years later, that same light or Spiritual Consciousness manifested Itself through a Hebrew rabbi named Jesus, transforming him into the Christ, the Son of God, the light of the world, the Savior.

The Western world has to grow spiritually and stop believing that Jesus is the only Son of God, and begin to accept that any human being who makes way for that Christ or light that he carries within will be able to spiritualize his consciousness and achieve *unity with God*.

It is vital importance for our spiritual development to recognize the universality of the Christ, who is the Spirit of God manifesting as your individual Spiritual Consciousness. And that Holy Spirit dwells not only within Jesus but also within each and every one of us. The conditioned human mind of the human being can never accept the true God. Moreover, for them it is a sacrilege to say that our true spiritual identity is God personified.

In John 10:34-36 it is narrated that when the Jews tried to stone Jesus for the "blasphemy" that being a man he was posing as God, Jesus answered them: **"It is not written in your law: 'I said you are gods'? If He called them gods to whom the word of God came, and the Scripture cannot be broken, why do they accuse of blasphemy the one whom the Father has sanctified and sent into the world? Why then do you accuse me of blasphemy because 'I said, I am God's Son'?"**

The Christ is not a person who came to this earth more than two thousand years. The man was Jesus but the Christ is the Spirit of God in man. In India it is called the Buddha-mind and in Japan Satori, and once that state of consciousness is reached there are no longer two powers operating. The Hebrew word Emmanuel has a similar meaning: "God with us." Where I am, God is, and where God is, I am. The whole of God is where I am.

Sadly, Christians believe that the Christ came for 33 years and has gone, and now they are waiting for his second coming. In reality, the second coming of Christ is the awakening of the Christ in each one of us. It is not the absurd concept of the return of Jesus Christ to earth "to judge the living and the dead," as the Nicene Creed states.

On the other hand, the Hebrews have never believed that the Messiah, the Christ has come, because they were waiting for a warrior to set them free of the Romans, and are still eagerly awaiting the kingdom of God and the Messiah. Both Christians and Hebrews alike are accepting in their consciousness the absence of the Christ and, consequently, they are kept separate from God.

There is nothing more destructive and harmful to the souls of the people who believe that the Christ belongs to a person, a sect, a church or a religion. What's more, it is a sacrilege to believe that the Christ is only in the saints and not in the sinners. Jesus is emphatic when he tells us in the Sermon on the Mount: **"Your Heavenly Father who makes the sun to rise on the evil and on the good, and send rain on the just and on the unjust"** (Matthew 5:45). This reveals to us that even if you find yourself in prison for a major sin or if you suffer from some sickness or you find yourself in poverty, the omnipresence of Christ is always at your fingertips waiting for you to open your conscience to him to free you from it.

Master Jesus also tells us: **"Whoever believes in me will do the works I have been doing, and they will do even greater things than these, because I am going to the Father"** (John 14:12). Here Jesus is telling us that all of us have the potential to become like him, and with a great humility tells us that we could even overcome it because it is not he who does the works but the Father who is within each one of us.

Continuing with this same concept, Master Jesus tells us in Matthew 5:48: **"Be perfect, therefore, as your heavenly Father is perfect."** You are the Christ-Self, you are the child of God, you are perfection itself and anything less than that is not you. That is why you can recognize it and want to overcome it; you want to lose sensuality and false appetites, because you, in your true identity, are the spiritual Son.

To reach that perfection that Jesus wanted for us has been denied to mankind for more than two thousand years by the religious organizations, Catholic and others, that refer to Jesus as the only Son of God, adulterating his original message. *That, undoubtedly, has been the biggest impediment to the spiritual development of humanity, both individually and collectively.*

On the other hand, accepting that Jesus is not the only Son of God does not take away any merit, quite the contrary. Of the billions of human beings who have passed through this planet, Master Jesus is the one has reached the highest Christ Consciousness, to the point of completely dissolving his humanity. He is the mystic among the mystics and it is the greatest inspiration of humanity to continue that difficult task, life after life, of "cleaning our window" or, as the oriental say, "to remove the onion skin" to reveal that wonderful splendor that is our Spiritual Consciousness.

To use the inspiration of the English poet and mystic Robert Browning (1812-1889), *"The Truth is within ourselves and we must open out a way where the imprisoned splendor may escape, instead of praying for it to enter."*

5.2 THE CONCEPT OF THE HOLY TRINITY

I must clarify that the Christ and the Holy Spirit are synonymous. On anywhere in the Bible where you read "Holy Spirit", you can read "The Christ" and vice versa. This radically changes the concept of Holy Trinity that Christians have. What's more, the words "Holy Trinity" are not in the Bible. However, for Christian theologians, the Holy Trinity is the central dogma of the nature of God, according to which God exists externally as three persons: Father, Son and Holy Spirit. For mystics, that concept has no validity because the Trinity does not refer to people but to functions.

To give us an example, the mystics invite us to think of a prism. God is the prism and works in three different ways. God functions as the Father, which is one side of the prism, and in that sense He is the Creator. On the other side of the prism, God functions as a series of synonyms: Holy Spirit, Christ, Savior, Teacher, Guide. We are going to call this second side of the prism, "the Christ." The function of the Christ is "God in action." It is the activity of the Father as Creator. The third side of the prism is God functioning as the "Son" as manifested form. So we have the Creator, the activity and the form. They are the three sides of the prism, the three functions in one. That conforms to the law of the universe which is *unity*.

In theology, the way they teach the Trinity is "God as three people". That is a humanization of God. In others words, it's a major nonsense.

The Trinity as three functions is the right thing: God as the Father (Creator), God as the Christ (God in action), and the third is God as the "Son." But not the Son as a human being because the Son is always spirit. *The Son is of the same substance as Father and the Christ. Everything is spiritual.*

5.3 THE DANGER OF FALLING INTO TEMPTATION

Continuing with the paradox of the duality of man, the Apostle Paul, for his part, points out that there are two people in each one of us, one person who is not under the law of God and the other who is the Son of God that has the Spirit of God dwelling in him. **"For I know that good itself does not dwell in me, that is, in my sinful nature. For I have the desire to do what is good, but I cannot carry it out. For I do not do the good I want to do, but the evil I do not want to do"** (Romans 7:18-19).

That is the truth about each of us human beings. Evil, or Satan, is neither in us nor has power over us because the only power is God, but it is always constantly present like *temptation. Evil is impersonal and works in us through fear or attraction.* We have to resist it because if we give in to temptation, we make it our own. We must always keep on guard, even more so if we are students of the truth that we are beginning to evolve in consciousness, and consequently, we are fragile like a seed that is beginning to germinate. We resist by holding on to the passages of the Bible that remind us to the Christ who dwells within us.

Temptation is always lurking, trying to take advantage and exploit our weaknesses. Sometimes we succumb to it and other times we managed to resist it. When it beats us, it is not because we are bad or because we have a good side and a bad side, but because we act under the *universal hypnotism* of which all human beings are victims.

Jesus himself, at the beginning of his gospel, was tempted three times, and three times rejected the temptations with a resounding **"Go away, Satan!."** But that hypnotism is so strong that it has come to bend people who have reached in some moments of his life great enlightenment. For example King David, author of the extraordinary 23rd Psalm: **"The Lord he is my shepherd, I shall not want...."** King

David, who had numerous wives and concubines, could not resist the temptation that presented itself in of a beautiful woman, Bathsheba, wife of one of his officers, and got her pregnant. Then tried to correct an evil with a greater evil, by send Bathsheba's husband to the front lines, where the fighting was harder, to get rid of him, putting into action, once again, the law of karma against him. **David married the widowed Bathsheba, but their first child died. David repented of his sins, and Bathsheba later gave birth to Solomon.**

The truth is that we are not tempted from outside but from inside of ourselves. We always project the temptation in such a way that it seems to be outside of us. We justify our fall by saying: "he tempted me", "she tempted me" or "that tempted me", but the reality is, as we have said previously, that *we contain in our consciousness everything that is externalized in our experience.*

An example that we see every day is that of the thousands of bank tellers in a city, very few are tempted by the money that passes through their hands. That tells you that it is not the money that tempts a person but the content of their conscience. If you are looking for health, money, love, loyalty, honesty, etc., those qualities are not found in the air or anywhere else, but in *your own consciousness. No one can have dominion over his life until he understands this great spiritual truth.*

Now, once we fully attain Christ Consciousness, the war between doing good or doing evil ends. No longer there are more temptations because you are living as a spiritual being, and you are seeing other people as spiritual beings. So, you only do to another what you like to be done to you, because you are the other. *In truth, there is no other!*

5.4 THE MESSAGE OF LOVE FOR THE FIRST TIME IS GIVEN TO THE WORLD

The Hebrew people had lived in slavery for four hundred years before Moses, without any access to education, culture or religion. It should also not surprise us that under those circumstances, they lacked moral sense. To these people, Moses presented a higher standard of living through the ten commandments. If these commandments, like other traditional customs, were obeyed, that person earned the title of "good

Hebrew"; but if the law was disobeyed, the violators were exposed to being stoned or excommunicated. No concept of love was included in those teachings. It was, strictly, a moral law.

The apostle John, in the prologue to his gospel, tells us: **"For the law was given by Moses, but Grace and Truth came by Jesus Christ "** (John 1:17) (capital letters are mine to emphasize those two words: Grace and Truth).

When we understand that the nature of God is *Love*, then we can understand the word *Grace*. Living under Grace means live under the gift or Love of God or Spiritual Consciousness, and that means to be maintained and sustained at all times by God. Then you not longer live by means of your job or salary or the food you eat, but due to another factor that now guides your life, which is Spiritual Grace; because it is written: **"Man shall not live on bread alone, but on every word that comes from the mouth of God"** (Matthew 4: 4).

When Jesus came, he taught a way of life much higher that the Mosaic law. He taught a spiritual life that is above our human opinions of what is good and what is bad; that is to say of the opposite pair: birth and death, health and disease, wealth and poverty, good and bad. A person can live in absolute obedience to the ten commandments and still be a long way from have a spiritual life, because spiritual life is looking at the world in a different way, without giving an opinion, without judging, without qualification of good or bad. In short, to look at it not with our physical senses, but with our spiritual sense. That is what is called, reaching the state of Grace, that is, *living in a state of Spiritual Consciousness beyond good and evil.*

Do not forget that Jesus was a Hebrew rabbi belonging to the organization of the Hebrew religion and, as such, was authorized to preach to the Jews in the synagogues. By the manuscripts of the Dead Sea discovered in 1946 we know that Jesus was admitted to the monastery of the Essenes when he was twelve years old, which according to the Hebrew custom, was the time when boys became men, and he went out to preach at the age of thirty. The Essenes were a Jewish sect that was not popular because they led a very austere life and its teachings were totally spiritual, rather than religious ceremonies and rituals.

Now this man, Jesus, receives enlightenment and begins to teach the men and women of his generation something entirely new and different. He teaches them to seek God within themselves instead of seeking Him in synagogues or temples, and frees them from the rituals and dogmas of the Hebrew religion.

For the high Jewish religious organization it was intolerable that one of them turned against the practices and beliefs established for so many years, including the annual pilgrimage to Jerusalem for the purpose of paying tithes and following rituals. Evidently, the teachings of Jesus posed a threat to the system of mental, physical and economic exploitation of the Jewish people in the hands of the Hebrew religious hierarchy. It is, then, when the special interests represented by the Sanhedrin or Supreme Council of the Jews, seeing themselves threatened, plan and achieve his crucifixion.

On the other hand, the Hebrew religious hierarchy had made the government of Caesar believe that Jesus Christ intended to dethrone them and establish his own government. From the human point of view that was absurd, especially coming from a person who preached *"not to resist evil"* and *"to love one's enemies."* Nevertheless, in the spiritual sense that was true. Jesus knew that *freedom is achieved within oneself, within our consciousness*, and that it does not depends on the clemency of dictatorial governments, since once you achieve the freedom of the soul, simultaneously you also achieve that of the mind, that of the body and even that of material wealth, because *our conscience is what manifests itself in our outer world.* Jesus was not going to settle for a spiritual realm that would leave humanity in a state of temporary slavery. *That is the greatest of Jesus' message: that you do not have to wait to die to live in the kingdom of God. The kingdom of God is available to everyone, here and now!*

Jesus brought to light that a spiritual life has nothing to do with the observance of rituals and external forms but with the state of consciousness carried out by the individual. *He preached a new dimension of life, not a religion.* A life of a higher consciousness, of a Spiritual Consciousness that requires as a preliminary step to eliminate, to tear out of your consciousness the old beliefs, since they are not compatible with his new teachings, because *"New wine is not poured into old wineskins."*

In the Sermon on the Mount, Jesus synthesizes the difference between Judaism and his new teaching, which was not yet known as Christianity, but as the teachings of a radical independent-thinking rabbi.

The Sermon on the Mount is the greatest message of *Love* that for the first time it is presented to the world. Never before has a message of *Love* been given to humanity. In it two diametrically opposed forms of life are presented: the **"You have heard that it was said ... "**, which is the way the world lives, and the **"but I say unto you ..."**, which is the new dispensation of life by Divine Grace and that it is impossible for a human being to achieve, unless he connects with the divine faculties within himself and lives through the spirit, and not through his body or his mind.

Jesus begins the Sermon on the Mount with the beatitudes, in which He indicates the essential characteristics of the people to enter the kingdom of God. In Matthew 5: 3-12 the eight beatitudes that Jesus spoke are collected:

1. **Blessed are the poor in spirit, for theirs is the kingdom of the heavens.** The phrase "poor in spirit" has a different connotation than what it means today. It means to those who are not satisfied with the things of this world; to those who have eliminated their egos and do not seek to climb social positions or gain power over others. They expect everything from God and nothing in the world.

2. **Blessed are they that mourn, for they shall be comforted.** On the spiritual dimension does not deny suffering and pain in the world. You have compassion, but you don't give it power. As we make the presence and power of God *real*, those who suffer around us will be released.

3. **Blessed are the meek, for they shall inheritance the earth.** The word meek has a mystical meaning that is "obedience" and means that only those who are in a state of total obedience to spiritual laws inherit God's land.

4. **Blessed are they which do hunger and thirst after righteousness, for they shall be filled.** As we reach a spiritual consciousness, this is expressed externally in a harmonious and fair way.

5. **Blessed are the merciful, for they shall obtain mercy.** We must not forget that our sins are forgiven to the extent that we forgive those who offend us.

6. **Blessed are the pure in heart, for they shall see God.** The pure in heart are those who have a pure or spiritual consciousness.

7. **Blessed are the peacemakers, for they shall be called the children of God.** We are peacemakers when we recognize the universality of the Christ.

8. **Blessed are they which are persecuted for righteousness' sake, for theirs is the kingdom of heaven.** For those who are starting on the spiritual path sometimes that beginning becomes evident with some negative experiences. The breaking with the old lifestyle can pose problems financial, emotional or physical. That is the meaning of phrase: **"He that finds his life shall lose it; and he that loses his life for my sake shall find it"** (Matthew 10:39). The human meaning of life must be sacrificed to give way to the spiritual meaning. For the early Christian martyrs, who went from being pagan to believing in one God, the persecution to which they were subjected was insignificant to the extent of their spiritual mission. From a human point of view, that does not makes sense. However, according to the enlightened ones, when you achieve contact with God what you receive more than makes up for what the world regards as a loss.

The rest of the message of the Sermon on the Mount we have mentioned in previous paragraphs and chapters when quoting Jesus, so it is not necessary to repeat it.

5.5 THE TEACHINGS OF JESUS CHRIST ARE ADULTERATED BY THE CHURCH

The first followers of Jesus Christ were called Judeo-Christians because they were Jewish followers of Christ; in fact, in those days only those who were Hebrews could become Christians. Eventually, Paul and Peter realized that Christian teachings were more than just a branch derived from Judaism. They were something unique, something totally different, and gradually it was accepted that to be a Christian was not necessary to be a Hebrew. Thus eventually, those teachings were extended to pagan or polytheistic peoples.

Christianity became the fastest growing religion of the time, while paganism was in frank declining. However, *in the middle of the second century the theologians of the Church they took over the leadership of Christianity, discarding mysticism,* and theological controversies arose that threatened the unity of the Christian Church. The controversies revolved fundamentally around the divinity of Jesus, since for some hierarchs of the Church, led by the priest Arius, *Jesus was the only Son of God but not God Himself,* while for others, led by Bishop Athanasius of Alexandria, *Jesus was the same God incarnate.* The leader of the latter group said publicly: *"Those who declare Jesus Christ inferior to God are worse than the Jews who they denied him, and that the Romans who crucified him."*

These differences among Christian theologians, evidently absurd and trivial to a spiritual conscience, vented in public reached so much pugnacity that the people on the street took sides with one group or the other to the point of forming hordes that in some extreme cases they even lynched bishops from the opposite side. This great theological conflict of the fourth century, known as *the Arian controversy,* struck the Christian world and produced the first ecumenical council of the Church. If you want to delve further into these historical events, I recommend you read the book "When Jesus Became God" by Professor Richard Rubenstein.

It's hard to imagine how the greatest doctrine of LOVE revealed to humanity, which includes loving our enemies and not resisting evil, could have degenerated into such acts of extreme violence. The same attitude that the Hebrew religious hierarchy had had against Jesus was now observed among the hierarchs of the Christian Church, who accused each other of heretics. Jesus knew that attitude very well of arrogant wise men of religious hierarchs when he said: **"I praise you, Father, Lord of heaven and earth, because you have hidden these things from the wise and learned, and revealed them to little children"** (Matthew 11:25).

The explanation of these terrible contradictions in behavior of human beings is that, to correctly understand and practice the spiritual principles revealed by the great enlightened ones of humanity, a Spiritual Consciousness is required. Once these enlightened beings and their more gifted disciples make their transition, the people who follow them interpret these spiritual principles in their own way, adapting them to a lower level of consciousness, which is the state of *mental consciousness*, and then to impose on others their views are willing to kill in the name of God.

In ancient times the State decided which religions were acceptable or legal. Judaism was considered a lawful religion under Julius Caesar. Any other faith was automatically declared illicit or illegal religion. That was the status of Christianity from the 60s AD once it became clear that Christianity was not the same as Judaism. The government could pursue, imprison and confiscate property from believers in Christ, such as indeed it did, but that, instead of destroying the Christians made them grow in number, while paganism was in decline.

Emperor Constantine I or Constantine the Great (272-337 AD), like all Roman emperors, was pagan. He particularly was a monotheistic worshiper of the god "Sun", but as a good politician he became interested in the growth of Christianity. The day before a major battle outside Rome, Constantine saw a sign in heaven: a cross accompanied by a legend: *"with this sign you will conquer."* Constantine had painted that sign on his banner and he won the battle, took over Rome and claimed that he had converted to Christianity. He publicly issued his edict of tolerance in AD 313, and the persecutions against Christians ceased, confiscated properties were returned and peace came.

For Emperor Constantine I, street violence between Christians was unacceptable, as it threatened the stability of the decaying Roman Empire. Furthermore, it was in the interests of the empire to have a unified and strong Church, so he summoned the First Council of Nicaea in the year 325, in order to achieve that unity. Constantine believed that God should be appeased with the correct worship and encouraged the idea among Christians that he "served their God." Constantine's role in trying to solve ecclesiastical disputes would be the beginning of a new relationship between the Roman Empire and the Christian Church. Then one of the strangest events in human history happened:

A new religion was established sponsored by the Roman Empire that adopted the ceremonies of the Egyptians and the pagans ornaments proper of the Gentiles, now sanctified by the Church, accepted Judaism as it is taught in the Old Testament, discarded all Christian teachings except the name of its revealer, and self-proclaimed representative of Christianity, being its greatest exponent the Catholic, Apostolic and Roman Church.

Jesus revealed to us a God of a totally different nature from of the Old Testament. Jesus taught us that sin is punished for sin itself and at no time does it refer to a God punisher. **"For in the same way you judge others, you will be judged"** Matthew (7:2), but it is not God who is going to judge you, but the law of **"For whatsoever a man sows, that shall he also reap"** (Galatians 6:7).

The organized Church embraced the punishing and implacable God of the Old Testament, something that is totally false and counterproductive, because evildoers soon discovered that there is no such God who punishes you for your sins. Just read the press or watch TV.

On the other hand, if the human being had been taught that sin is punished by sin itself, which is the interpretation of Jesus of the law of cause and effect or karma; and that that law, that operates within each one of us, knows our most intimate thoughts and feelings and, consequently, we cannot escape from it, then, the human being would have been prepared for the highest teachings of Jesus Christ.

5.6 THE REVELATION OF GOD'S NAME

The Bible, in Exodus 3, tells us how God is presented to Moses on Mount Sinai and entrusts him with the task of bringing the people of

Israel out of Egypt. **"And God said to Moses: 'I AM WHO I AM'. This is what you are to say to the Israelites: 'I AM has sent me to you'"** (Exodus 3:14). From that moment on, Moses reached the experience of God that goes beyond words and thoughts. It is what the mystics tell us that God must be *experienced* and that it is not enough just to think about it. At that moment, Moses acquired a *new conscience*, which is what allowed him to finally liberate the Hebrew people from the horror of slavery.

Of all the peoples of antiquity, the Hebrew people were the ones who prayed with greatest devotion and faith to one God. However, that God "up there" never entered the scene for hundreds of years while the Hebrew people lived under the iron hand of Pharaoh. God came to enter scene only when Moses achieved *God realization*. In others words, *God came into action through enlightened consciousness of Moses*.

Here it should be noted that Moses never taught the truth to his people, considering it very dangerous that human beings declared that "I am God", and gave his people substitute names of God, such as Yahweh, Jehovah, Elohim, Lord among others, but never gave them the true name of God: I. Only the highest ranking priests were allowed to pronounce the name of God once a year and only when they were alone in the sanctuary more sacred to all sanctuaries: the "ark of the covenant." That was the only time when they were allowed to pronounce the word: "I."

Later, King Solomon learned that great truth, and came to be the wisest and richest man of his time. Solomon knew the secret of life and that was the secret of his greatness. Solomon wanted to share his secret with others, but he set a high price that went beyond studies and religious practices. It required a state of Spiritual Consciousness that allows receiving the Truth without to try to be gods. Unfortunately, Solomon did not find someone to reveal his secret and that is the reason why the Truth was lost for many centuries in the Western world.

5.7 WHO AM I?

There is a very old tale about a great spiritual master who knocks at the gates of heaven to enter paradise. Then God asks:

"Who is there?", "Who is knocking?" The teacher responds: I am, to which God responds: I'm very sorry, but there is no space in heaven. Go and come another day. The good man, surprised by the rejection, leaves confused. After many years of meditation and reflection on that strange reception, he returns and knocks on the door again. God asks him the same question and he gives a similar answer. Once again, God tells him that there is no space in heaven since it is totally full at that time. In the following years, the teacher deepens his meditation and goes deep into his consciousness. Long after, he goes and knocks on the gates of heaven for the third time. Again God asks him: "Who is there?", and this time his answer is: You are. And the doors are opened, while God tells him: Come in, there has never been room for me and you."

When you say "I", or when I say "I", the next question is: Who am I?, What am I?, What do I do here?. That is the great mystery of life. We know very well that you and I as people are not God. We know our weaknesses and our infirmities, and we definitely know that we are not gods. *No human being is God.* **God is not a man** (Numbers 23:19). However, *I am God, or all revelations of the world's mystics have been wrong.*

When a person says "I", whether it is "I so-and-so", he is referring to his person in the human sense, such as his sex, his race, his age, his weight, his education, his occupation, and, finally to all the other concepts that he has about himself. Now, when you manage to get rid of all those concepts that you have of yourself, remains your true "I". That "I", which is neither your body nor your mind, neither masculine nor feminine, and that is free of all concepts, is your true Self. It is not that you and I are God, but rather that the "I" within me and the "I" within you, not by saying it but by hearing it within ourselves is what makes the statement *"Father and I are one"*, true. That "I" is the internal being of the individual. That "I" is the soul of the individual. That "I" is our true identity. That "I" is God.

In studying the mystical and philosophical revelations of the world, we do not find a deeper truth than that, and it is precisely due to its depth, that truth has not been able to keep throughout the history of mankind. Whenever there has been a teacher who has revealed it to us, very few have been the disciples who have understood it, and once the master and his closest disciples have made their transition, the teaching has been lost.

Unfortunately for humanity, what has always prevailed is a false personal sense of "I". *Contemplating a false sense of "I" is the cause of all problems in the world.* Give up the me-me or the me-you and you won't find any discord in the world.

Master Jesus understood that the solution to all the problems of the human being, individual and collective, was to achieve a correct sense of 'I', and proceeded to reveal to the Hebrew people what had not been done on the face of the earth. He addressed the people on the street, the townspeople, the masses and told them the Truth: *that God's kingdom is within you, and God's name is I.* **"I and my Father are one"** (John 10:30); **"He that has seen me has seen the Father"** (John 14: 9); **"I am the way, the truth, and the life"** (John 14: 6). And so, for revealing the truth, he was crucified.

Today, Truth can be revealed openly, in clear and direct language, as I am doing here, without fear of being crucified. In that sense we have made some progress. But sadly, that Truth does not produce a regeneration in people's lives. It does not produce the spiritual fruit that is to be expected. The reason is that *the Truth cannot be demonstrated intellectually*. People first have to develop spiritually and then receive the message from within their own conscience in order to demonstrate the Truth. When the message is received by the person from outside, directed to his mind or intellect, there is not demonstration. *However, knowing the truth with your mind is a good start, since it is through the mind that you get to the consciousness.* Furthermore, according to rational thinking "You have to understand to believe."

Joel S. Goldsmith was offered in 1960 ten million dollars to broadcast on television throughout the United States his mystical message "The Infinite Way", but he declined the offer because he considered that the message in itself has no power. *The power is in the enlightened consciousness of the person.* The world has had great mystics through all its history: Moses, Lao-Tzu, Buddha, Shankara, Isaiah, Elijah, Jesus Christ, John, Paul, and many other modern mystics who have followed that same trajectory. In addition, the world has had many sacred scriptures, both of the East and of the West, and are the most widely printed books today. However, all those enlightened people and those books have not been able to get the world out of the *universal hypnotism* in which they find themselves and elevate it to a state of spiritual consciousness. However, thousands of people have benefited from the revelations of the mystics and have managed to dehypnotize themselves by spiritualizing their consciousness.

The light that illuminates us today is the result of the set of rays of light that the spiritual prophets of the world have contributed to us for thousands of years. All those spiritual masters consecrated their lives to let us know the Truth, which is what has led us to the present state of consciousness.

Sadly, this is not a message that can be accepted by most people who live on a level of *mental consciousness* almost exclusively. Spiritual Truth is so absurd to a human that his conditioned mind refuses to accept it. Remember what the apostle Paul tells us in I Corinthians 2:14: **"But the natural man does not receive the things of the Spirit of God, for they are foolishness to him; nor can he know them, because they are spiritually discerned."**

For the human being, all that is achieved in the world is from outside activities, including the search for Truth. They try to reach it in religious organizations and in mountains and sacred temples, even though Jesus made it clear to us that the kingdom of God is within us. That is the reason why Jesus advises in Matthew 7:6: **"Do not give dogs what is sacred; do not throw your pearls to pigs. If you do, they may trample them under their feet, and turn and tear you to pieces."**

A person with spiritual discernment, when he looks around does not see God and man but only God expressed, manifested as an individual being. God is our invisible Self. There is no God outside in space. The only God that exists is within ourselves, as the fable of the gods of Mount Olympus points out, and *all you have to do to find it is expand the content of your consciousness. Then you can make the Kingdom of God real within you.*

If I want to know you and you want to know me, we cannot do it by looking at our bodies or by digging into our minds, because your body and your mind are something that you possess to perform your functions on earth, but none of them are you. In order to know each other, you will have to enter into communion with my soul and I with yours, in meditation, until we understand that we are both children of the same Father, members of the great family of God. We are all branches of the tree of life, all connected to the tree, which is the source and substance of all lives, without any branch depending on the other. This life of ours is eternal, incorporeal and infinite, maintained and sustained by Spiritual Consciousness or God. And so we get to know that **"The Lord is my shepherd, I shall not want ..."** (Psalm 23). But as long as we keep in our conscience, consciously or unconsciously, that we are human beings and not spiritual beings, we will stand outside the gates of heaven with no hope of getting in.

What keeps us separate from God is the sense of separation, perception of duality, not duality itself, because there is no such duality. Let's never forget that there are not two of us. There is not a human being and a spiritual being. Let's also not forget that there is no a material universe and a spiritual universe. There is only one universe and that is the spiritual universe. There is only one I, and that is our spiritual being.

CHAPTER 6

Meditation

6.1 THE CONCEPT OF PRAYER

The word "pray" comes from the Latin "orare", which means "to speak." The dictionary defines the word "pray" as "to make a request to God". That concept is shared by the general public but, sadly, it is a misconception of prayer that comes to us from thousands of years of pagan practices that we have recorded in the subconscious.

Praying is not asking something of an infinite intelligence that loves us, but to listen to what that infinite intelligence tells us. Jesus, in his instructions on how to pray, tells us in Matthew 6:7-8: **"And when you pray, do not keep on babbling like pagans, for they think they will be heard because of their many words. Do not be like them, for your Father knows what you need before you ask Him."**

Words are not necessary to draw you closer to God. What's more, they are an impediment. There is a tale of a girl whose mother tells her to pray, and she sits quietly and begins in a low voice to murmur the alphabet: "a, b, c,...." Her mother asks: "What are you doing?." And she replies: "Praying, but since I don't know the right words to address God, I say all the letters of the alphabet so that God can puts them together."

Jesus continues to instruct us in how to pray and in Matthew 6:6 we He says: **"But when you pray, go into your room, close the door and** pray to your Father, who is unseen. Then your Father, who sees what is done in secret, will reward you."** In mystical language, that means close your mind to the outside world, enter the depth of your conscience and listen carefully when you are going to be in communion with God.

From the mystical point of view, *prayer and meditation are synonyms*, and consist of three important phases: *the first phase* is generally known as *"meditation"* and consists of spiritualizing your thoughts with spiritual phrases. There must be a total surrender of our desires, worries, fears and concepts. We cannot pretend to use meditation to ask God for something. The just looking for God to get something is a barrier. **"Not my will, but yours be done"** (Luke 22:42). Going to God without any desire largely eliminates the personal 'I', because it is only the personal "I" that can have desires or purposes. We go to God only to receive the Spiritual Blessing.

When waking up every morning, during the day and before going to bed every night, sit still and start the morning with a meditation in which you contemplate God and the works of God. Do not forget that one of the great phrases of the Bible is: **"In all your ways submit to Him, and He will make your paths straight"** (Proverbs 3:6). That means that from the moment you wake up in the morning, your first thought should be something like: *"Thank you, Father, for your eternal presence in me and for going before me preparing the way in this glorious day that you have created."* Making a habit of meditation at the beginning of your day is very important, because it prepares you to serve and keep God in mind that day.

Then it is recommended to focus on a phrase from Scripture, the one that most catches your attention. You can choose any of those mentioned in this book or any other phrase from the Bible. Focus on just one and reflect on it. Mystics have different ways to ease their minds. The mystical Lorraine Sinkler tells in her book "The Alchemy of Awareness" that she spent two years meditating several times a day with the phrase of Jesus: **"The Father and I are one."** In that extraordinary phrase, God establishes the relationship that God, the Father, and God, the Son, have always been *one* for eternity. Begin by asking yourself: "Who am I? If I lose a foot, would I feel less? If I lose a leg, will I feel less myself? If I lose both legs, am I still me? And so on, until you see clearly that if you lose your whole body you would continue being you. When you make your transition, you will have the experience to know that you are not in your body but that your body is yours. You will be able to see your family and friends watching over your body, dress and makeup, while your true "I" will wonder when the human race will awaken from its hypnotic state and will come out of that primitive and pagan practice, accepting the spiritual reality.

Meditate each time for a short period of time. In the beginning, if you get to meditate for a minute or two, it is remarkable. When your mind begins to intrude and fidget, suspend your meditation. The kingdom of God cannot be attained by force. That is a process without mental or physical effort and without anxiety; otherwise you are defeated before starting.

The purpose of this first phase is to learn to focus the mind on a single spiritual idea and understand it deeply. Obviously, this is a purely *mental* activity. Once you can focus on a spiritual phrase for as long as you want without your mind getting in the way, interrupting with alien thoughts, then you are ready for the next step or the second phase. According to the mystics, this first phase can take you from one to three years, depending on your dedication and the practice of spiritual principles, as well as your current level of consciousness.

Under no circumstances should the beginner sit down to meditate for a long period of time trying to "whiten" his mind. The *"Silence"*, referred to by mystics, is only achieved when you have an *unconditioned mind*; that is, *when you have reached a Spiritual Consciousness.*

The second phase is called *"contemplation"*, which we will analyze later and consists of abandoning all intellectual effort and being aware of the "Presence." It is considered the door of entrance to communion.

The third phase is what is known as *"true prayer"* or *"communion"*, which is when we get rid of our humanity, beyond words and thoughts, and we achieve *God realization. Realization means making real in our consciousness the presence and power of God. It is what gives us the experience of God.* This is the hardest thing to achieve, even for the more advanced in the difficult art of meditation. It is unlikely that you reach such a high degree of meditation, unless you lead a monastic life.

Thus, *the ultimate purpose of meditation is to achieve a conscious realization of our unity with God.* Jesus called that presence and power

"Father": **"The Father that dwells in me, he does the works"** (John 14:10). The apostle Paul, using a different term, tells us: **"I live, yet not I, but the Christ lives in me"** (Galatians 2:20) and, also, **"I can do all things through Christ who strengthens me"** (Philippians 4:13). But whatever the name used, be it God, Father, Christ or the Infinity Invisible, it will not be found neither in mountains nor in sacred temples nor in religious organizations but in the depth of our own consciousness. *The climax of the meditation is achieved when direct contact with God is made.* It's not about having conversations or making repeated statements about God. *It is a true fact to be able to make personal and real contact with God and hear* **"A still small voice"** (I Kings 19:12). That is what mystics call the experience of God. Is the definition of *mysticism*, since this can be defined as *the conscious contact with God or Spiritual Consciousness.*

Due to the noises from the outside world, we do not hear the *"still small voice"* that God is constantly whispering inside us. God is eternally transmitting His infinite wisdom, but to be able to hear it we have to be on the same spiritual frequency, rather than the mental frequency in which we human beings find ourselves. It's something like a radio or television program that we cannot tune into because it is not on the correct frequency. The spiritual frequency is *silence*, and it is for that reason that we must learn to calm the mind beyond the words and thoughts in order to receive the blessings of His Presence.

Be careful not to be fooled by the mind. Some people say they hear voices and have visions that they interpret as an "experience with God." However, there are no fruits but exhaustion and confusion. That is the big difference between a mental activity and a spiritual activity. **"By their fruit you will recognize them"** (Matthew 7:16).

On the other hand, sometimes at an unexpected moment, an idea comes to us that is the perfect answer to a problem that we have, but because it does not come to us when we are meditating, we do not recognize it for what it is: the fruit of our meditation. As we are fulfilling our part of daily meditation, the answer can come to us at any time without waiting for it.

6.2 THE ART OF MEDITATION

Joel S. Goldsmith is credited with having restored the meditation practice in the Western world. In 1956 he wrote the book "The Art of Meditation", and like all art, it is based on laws. Just as the aspiring artist must first discover the laws that govern his art and then, after many years of practice, reach that level of inspiration that will transform him into an artist; in the same way, people aspiring to a spiritual life must begin by knowing the spiritual laws contained in the letter of truth, which is all that you have read so far in this book. Only after putting them into practice for years in their daily lives, and by meditating many times a day, they will be able to reach the *realization or Divine Grace*.

There is no problem that true meditation cannot solve. Become adept at meditation by practicing it constantly, whether you are driving or performing any other activity. Once that Divine Grace has been achieved to a great extent, she assumes the command of our lives. We no longer live on bread alone but by that internal Grace that translates into tangible effects, such as satisfying relationships, abundance of health, prosperous businesses and creativity. But we must attain inner Grace before the things of this world can be added to us.

Despite how difficult it is to master the art of meditation, there is nothing mysterious about it. However, there are many myths that we are going to dispel of immediately:

1. *Proper posture*. In the East it is customary to meditate sitting on the floor, cross-legged. In that position they are comfortable, but we in the West we are not comfortable in that position. Let's not forget that in meditation all our attention should be focused on God and in God's affairs. Consequently, it is very important that our body is in a comfortable position so that it does not distract our attention. It is recommended to sit comfortably with your back straight, the chest forward, breathing gently. Meditation is a conscious act in which you have to be alert awaiting instructions, so one should avoid falling asleep. However, in some state of meditation

sleep may come, but such a sleep is not a loss of consciousness but a continuation of the activity of consciousness.

2. *Diet.* People often wonder if there is a special diet that increases our spiritual capacity; if for example, certain foods such as meat should be avoided. We tend to believe that something we do in the outer world will help us in our spiritual development. The truth is, as we develop spiritually, this new consciousness is changing our habits and our way of life. We must train ourselves to pause briefly before eating or drinking to recognize and be thankful that what we eat and drink comes from the infinite and invisible Consciousness.

3. *Psychic experiences.* We have already pointed out that in no mystical literature refers to psychic phenomena as a spiritual experience. All of this is part of the *universal mind* where each mind is connected with all the other minds, but there's no spirituality at all of it. Beginners who try to achieve silence with long hours of meditation are inviting psychic forces to dominate their mind with undesirable results.

4. *Period of time.* It is not necessary to meditate for a specific time period. When meditation begins to be a physical or mental effort, stop. The kingdom of God is not taken by force. The best way to practice meditation is trying to quiet your mind several times a day for very short periods. At first, one or two minutes of meditation three times a day are enough. It is important that you do it upon waking up in the morning before starting your day, then during the day, and finally before bed.

5. *Inner silence.* The hardest thing about meditation is keeping thoughts in only one direction. As we close our eyes in an attempt to meditate, we discover something akin to a steam boiler made up of thoughts within us. Actually, it is not our fault but in large part, it is the fault of the fast pace of modern life, which

has caused all our attention to be focused on material things and external people. That makes all kinds of thoughts flash through our minds. But do not worry about them, because they are not your thoughts but of the world. Our minds are like antennas that pick up all the transmissions in the environment, but if you don't pay attention to them in a few weeks they will disappear due to lack of attention. Only if you accept them as yours and resist them, they persist. If we ignore them, eventually they will leave us in peace. In meditation we must be very patient in our attempt to achieve inner peace. As long as we keep in our mind that some things are good and some are bad, our minds will be restless, but the moment we can look at people and conditions as neither good nor bad and surrender all adjectives, then our thoughts stop and the mind quiets down. At this point this becomes an instrument through which God manifests Himself. The human mind, that thinking and reasoning mind, does not need to be eliminated. She has her place. It is not Consciousness, but it is the entrance and exit door to Consciousness. It is through the *unconditioned mind* that we receive the knowledge and wisdom of the Spiritual Consciousness or God.

6.3 CONTEMPLATIVE MEDITATION

The word "contemplation" comes from two Latin words: *con* and *templum*, which means *"to join the temple."* We go to that temple within ourselves, where our Father dwells. Paul tells us in I Corinthians 3:16: **"Do you not know that you are the temple of God, and that the Spirit of God dwells in you?"**

In fact, *the contact has always been established, because it is impossible to be separated from God because we would not exist. We do not have to seek the kingdom of God but simply recognize it because the kingdom of God is already within ourselves, saints and sinners. What we have to do is be receptive enough, through meditation, to consciously reconnect with our Father.* It's that easy and yet that difficult. For the human being, the things that are worthwhile in life are achieved with great effort, but simple things, such as loving your neighbor, animals and plants that cost nothing and bring you closer to the spiritual world, are ignored.

They are not our struggles in life to raise our family that makes us worthy of the Creator. Jesus tells us that we should cultivate the simplicity, humility and innocence of children if we want inherit the kingdom of God. In the Jewish culture of that time, children were not taken into account socially because they were considered immature and incapable of knowing the law, necessary to achieve salvation. The disciples, according to their culture and mentality of the time, rebuke those who had brought the children to Jesus to touch him. But Jesus called them to him and said: **"Let the little children come to me, and do not hinder them, for the kingdom of God belongs to such as these. Truly I tell you, anyone who will not receive the kingdom of God like a child will never enter it"** (Luke 18:16-17).

Now, before entering the temple of God who dwells within us, we need to be *clean of conscience*. We must perform a conscious act of forgiveness, considered one of the greatest laws revealed by Jesus Christ. **"For if you forgive other people when they sin against you, you heavenly Father will also forgive you. But if you do not forgive others their sins, your Father will not forgive your sins."** (Matthew 6:14-15). Consequently, before we enter the temple of God that is within us, we must make a pause and forgive all those people who have offended us in our life and also forgive ourselves. Now we are aware that any sin that we have committed or of which we have been victims is a consequence of the spiritual ignorance of the human being, for not knowing their true identity.

As we have already said, in the first phase of meditation we focus on a single spiritual phrase and reflect on it. That is a mental process, because a phrase by its nature is intellectual. Now, let's erase that spiritual phrase from the mind. We are going to "clear the mind," which is an intermediate step between meditation and contemplation. We achieve that with a mental image. Imagine, for example, a beautiful sunset on the seashore, with the waves in motion reaching the shore and retreating. Or a full moon on a clear night, reflected in the clean water of a lake surrounded by trees. Or any other beautiful image you can think of. That is your mind and your image, and you are visualizing that picture in your mind. You can do with it as you please. Now introduce a strong wind and you will see the waves rise or the trees move. Increase the force of the wind even more. Remember that they are your mind and your image and that you can do with them whatever you want. Now go appeasing the wind until nothing moves in the image; everything is calm and, at that moment, you freeze the picture. By freezing the image you are controlling the mind. Now you can calm her down. This method was taught to us by the mystic Barbara Muhl in a private class I attended in 1992, in Burbank, California.

Mrs. Muhl also taught us a faster way to get straight to God, something that is not found in any books. Remember that God gave us five physical senses that are those that allow our physical contact with the world around us. God also gave us a sixth sense, which is the mind, the instrument of intellectual knowledge and communication with the outside world. In our spiritual ignorance, we try many times using the mind to reach God, even though it was never designed for that. Consequently, by these means it is impossible get to God. It's like trying to read a book with your sense of smell. It is the wrong tool. You can only use the abilities that God gave you what they were designed for! For communication with God, we use a seventh faculty which is *Consciousness*. That is not another tool like the other six that were given to us by God. *That is the tool of God!* Also known as the seventh faculty, Spiritual faculty or faculty of the Soul, which is the one that should be used to make contact with God.

Mrs. Muhl tells us to do the following exercise:

1. Close your eyes and "be aware of your ears". There are no words no thoughts. Where is your mind? You are aware of your ears and you didn't use your mind because you are without words or thoughts. You are showing that you have another faculty, which is not the mind, and which in English is called *awareness* and in Spanish *consciencia*. Now increase awareness of your ears. What about your ears now? Now you are more aware of your ears because that is exactly what the word *increase* means. Now you know that this faculty not only does and goes where you order it to go but also increases when you ask it. It is a faculty that is, in a way, under your control; a lot more than the mind which is like a wild horse without control.

2. Now, close your eyes and "be aware of your knees". What happened to your ears? They disappeared! Did you realize that? That wonderful faculty not only does and goes where you order, but you are not aware of two things at the same time, and this is very important.

3. Let's go back to the previous point and increase being aware of your knees. We are addressing to *the Spiritual Faculty or Faculty of the Soul*. What makes that Faculty obey us? *"I and my Father are one, but my Father is greater that I."* This is our *Spiritual Faculty* that could ignore us if It wanted to, but It doesn't. Why doesn't It if It is omnipotent, omnipresent and omniscient? Because Its nature is *love* and it is *"The will of the Father to give us his kingdom."*

4. Now, "be aware of I." Of that spiritual I that is your true self. Visualize that Christ or light illuminating your current realized consciousness. Visualize that light covering your body, your family, your friends, your job, your country, in short, everything that you are. Now increases to a superlative degree the awareness of that light that expands, again and again, until it envelops the universe in its entirety, transforming into the Spiritual Consciousness or God. Visualize your consciousness merging with the Spiritual Consciousness or God. With great humility, You will be able to feel that *"The Father and I are one."* Now you can say humbly like the young Hebrew: **"Speak, Lord, for your servant is listening"** (I Samuel 3: 9) and keep your ear attentive as if you were to listen to the *"the still small voice"* that mystics living in the fourth dimension have heard, even though they temporarily remain in our human world. Once in the Temple, you will feel the Presence of God. You will know that you are in the Temple, because the Presence will be there and you will know it, and you will feel it. God is infinite and it will certainly be possible to announce to each one of us in different

ways. You will be able to verify that the Presence has been there for the fruits.

6.4 HISTORY OF MEDITATION

Contemplative meditation or prayer, as it was known in the Antiquity, was discovered and practiced in the East thousands of years ago. For Oriental people it is something natural, because they have a culture of meditation, contemplation and silence. Then, that practice spread to the Western world, but its true purpose of consciously realizing our unity with God was derailed when the human being began to use meditation as a means to reach through the mind the things of this world: health, money, love or power. Actually, the role of mind was changed from a passive role to an active role. In other words, *mind power* was preferred that is under our dominion to control others, to *spiritual power* that is achieved through meditation but cannot be used to control others.

The great mystery of meditation is that it is not a means to obtain the things of this material world from the divine center of our own being. Moreover, the mere desire to obtain something prevents meditation. At no time can we consider God as an instrument through which we can get something. Your only wish should be to reach communion with God with purity of intention. In verses from the 8th century Sufi mystical poet Rabi'a: *"Oh my God! If I adore you for fear of hell, burn me in it; and if I adore you for the hope of paradise, exclude me from it. But if I adore you only for yourself, do not deprive me of your eternal beauty."*

Meditation is rare in the Western world. However, it was not absent in the first centuries of the Christian Church. Sadly, in the 17th century Emperor Justinian I the Great (483-565), convinced that the unity of the Roman Empire required of the unity of faith represented by the Orthodox Catholic, decreed the total destruction of the Neoplatonist Christian schools that professed the idea that the individual can make direct contact with God. That political decision of the emperor Justinian, venerated as a saint of the Catholic Church, was very convenient to the interests of a controlling and expanding Church, but a terrible blow to the spiritual maturity of the individual. The Catholic Church, once again, imposing itself as indispensable between the individual and God. The Church jealously guarded it role as intercessor to the point of accusing as heretics and executing in the name of God those who offer the freedom of spirit that the contemplative path signified, in the face of absolute control of the Church over its parishioners. One of the victims was the Spanish priest and mystic Miguel de Molinos (1628-1696), who in 1675 wrote his *Spiritual Guide*, a work that was welcomed with great enthusiasm by *Quietism*, a mystical movement that emerged in the Catholic Church, especially in Spain, France and Italy. Ten years after its publication, the *Spiritual Guide* was banned by Pope Innocent XI, and Father Molinos was arrested along with some of his disciples in 1685. He was accused of heresy and died in the prisons of the Inquisition nine years later. Numerous adherents of Quietism ended up at the bonfires of the Holy Office.

In the last forty-four years a movement has appeared of monks and laity founded in 1977 by the English Benedictine monk John Main, which focuses on the practice of meditation. That movement is today called the World Community for Christian Meditation and is present in more than fifty countries. The meditation that they teach and practice is much like transcendental meditation of the Maharashi Mahesh Yogi that has spread the whole world, and both meditations consist of repeating until fatigue a mantra for thirty minutes, twice a day, in order to achieve Silence through the mind's daze. But Silence is not an absence of mental sounds. It is not through fooling the mind that we reach Silence. *Silence is a stage of consciousness. In fact, we reach silence only when we have reached the stage of Spiritual Consciousness.* Additionally, all those meditations offered to the public through the media are just another method of relaxation in order to reduce the stress of modern life. They have nothing to do with the development of a spiritual awareness. Instead of trying to quiet the mind to eliminate thoughts that cause us stress using a hypnotizing mantra, we use the mind to inspire ourselves in passages of scripture or other spiritual writings that help raise awareness to feel the presence of God.

The true meditation, to which we refer here, is an extremely difficult practice to master, even for those who are living a spiritual life. Joel S. Goldsmith, in his book *The Art of Meditation*, tells us his own experience that led him to make that first contact or click, which produced an indescribable feeling of that presence within him. He tells us that he achieved his first contact with God, that only lasted a second, after eight months of meditating ten times a day. That first contact was an extraordinary revelation, because Joel had no knowledge that such contact with God was possible, even though he was already doing spiritual healings. Joel tells us that what kept him attached to that search was an irreducible conviction that he could touch God if he went to the deepest part of his consciousness. It should be clarified that a person can have the gift of spiritual healing without knowing how it happens. Joel continues in his book telling us that after that first contact it took a week to get a second contact of another second of duration, and many other days for a third contact; until, finally, he got to establish daily contacts of up to a minute lasting each time, what seemed like an eternity. The mystic Barbara Muhl tells us in her book *The Royal Road to Reality* that, after twenty-five years of studying metaphysics and mysticism in Eastern and Western schools, it took her two and a half years, this time under the spiritual guidance of Joel Goldsmith, to achieve her first contact with God.

6.5 WHEN CAN I REALIZE GOD WITHIN ME?

To the question of: How long will it take me to establish contact at will with the Father within me? The answer to that is something very personal. There is a spiritual path for each person and each one walks it alone. No one can reach "heaven" or nirvana with the conscience of another. There are a few people who, due to their previous experiences, are prepared for this path and their progress is pretty fast. The purity of consciousness that they have developed in previous lives makes their advance to Spiritual Consciousness gradual and harmonious with very few ups and downs. But for most of us the road is long and difficult and full of ups and downs. However, if we persevere, we find that after the downs come new heights.

There is a tale from Zen Buddhism that illustrates the dedication that requires "living" a spiritual life:

It is said that a Zen student walked with his teacher through the bank of a stream and anxiously asked repeatedly "Master, When am I going to meet God? When will I reach my enlightenment?" The master, his patience exhausted, without further ado grabbed him by neck and threw him into the stream, keeping his head under the water as the student struggled to breathe. Then he said calmly: "When you want to know God with the same strength and desire with which you wanted to breathe, then you will know it."

Sooner or later, in this life or the next, each one of us will get that intense desire to reach the illumination. A distinction must be made between "living" a spiritual life, which is what mystics lead, and the long spiritual journey back to our Father's house that we are starting. But do not be discouraged, because with each meditation we move slowly but inexorably towards our goal of reaching the stadium of Spiritual Consciousness.

Many people who know *the letter of truth* and are on the spiritual path, when they have a problem that comes directly to them or their relatives, they forget the spiritual teachings and react like pagans by pleading with God to solve the problem. That is a consequence of conditioning that we have been victims of for thousands of years, both in this life as in all the previous ones. Intellectually we believe in omnipotence, omnipresence and omniscience of God but not with enough conviction to depend on it. That is the difference between *intellectualization* and *realization*. However, it is very important that we make an effort to act as if we had the conviction of spiritual principles. Putting in practice these principles is what will move us forward on the spiritual path.

Meditation is the method we use to build a new consciousness. Of course, we first have to empty our consciousness of all those beliefs of separation and duality to which we have been conditioned for generations, to make room for the new spiritual concepts expressed here. It is the new consciousness that Jesus speaks of, which is indispensable for the seed of spirituality to germinate and bear fruit. Even when we do not reach the *climax* of meditation in this life, when we manage to put our mind on the affairs of God, or what is called *contemplative meditation*, we already begin to experience a change of consciousness that will manifest itself positively in our outside world. We will receive the fruit of our change in consciousness very soon.

And finally, keep in mind that the Truth is not disputed when you are starting your spiritual path. Truth is pondered, meditated within oneself. The spiritual seed that you are beginning to sow in your conscience you have to protect it and water it daily so that it can grow and become stronger. Paul tells us that *"the things of God are for the human being foolishness and cannot understand them"* and Jesus advises us *"not to cast our pearls to pigs, lest they be trampled on"*. So keep this knowledge in a sacred and secret way so that it can germinate and bear fruit in your life.

At the beginning of this book, I invited you to undertake the most interesting and important trip of your life. This is a different journey because it is not done in time or space. *It is a journey in conscience.* Climate changes and other natural phenomena that we are currently experiencing, such as tsunamis, earthquakes, hurricanes, floods and village fires, with victims in alarming proportions, make us think that we are experiencing a potentially dangerous transition stage. A large number of scientists think that what we are experiencing, product of our excessive consumption of raw materials and an indifferent attitude towards the delicate ecological balance, it is only an announcement of major and profound changes on the horizon. Only the human being will be able to determine if this new cycle represents a new age of spiritual growth or other cataclysm followed by an age of darkness, as has happened in the past. The final result will be determined by a single fundamental factor: *consciousness. It will be the collective consciousness of the human being that will determine, once again, the future of humanity.*

Personally, you have nothing to fear. Insofar that you stay on the spiritual path, **"A thousand may fall at your side, ten thousand at your right hand; but it will not come near you"** (Psalms 91:7). The Spiritual development is something entirely individual. We can't pretend to save the world, not even our own family, because we are different levels of *realized consciousness* and to each one the desire for their spiritual development will come in due time. That is something out of our reach. However, by ascending spiritually you will be able to *silently* help the people in your family circle and friends, who are in tune with your consciousness, to raise their vibration levels. In that way, we can help others in the *great transition from homo sapiens to homo spirit.*

PSALM 23
THE LORD IS MY SHEPHERD
A PSALM OF DAVID

1. The Lord is my shepherd; I shall not want

2. He maketh me to lie down in green pastures; he leadeth me beside the still waters.

3. He restoreth my soul; he guideth me in the paths of righteousness for his name's sake.

4. Yea, though I walk through the valley of the shadow of death, I will fear no evil; for thou art with me; thy rod and thy staff, they comfort me.

5. Thou preparest a table before me in the presence of mine enemies; thou hast anointed my head with oil; my cup runneth over.

6. Surely goodness and lovingkindness shall follow me all the days of my life; and I shall dwell in the house of the Lord for ever.

This is a completely new concept of prayer. In this prayer there is no supplication to God for anything. Note that from the beginning to the end there is no attempt to seek the goodness of God. God cannot be used. There is only the recognition that because God is my shepherd, my friend, my protector, my support, I lack nothing. There is no search for health or wealth because "He makes me lie down in green pastures and leads me to still waters." There is no doubt, there is trust, there is security. And if at some point in our lives we have to go through periods of trials and tribulations, "I will fear no evil for you're with me." This Psalm brings a deeper realization of the great truth that harmony already is. It is a matter of opening our consciousness.

This is truly a miracle of prayer.

PRAYER TO THE FATHER

Thank you Father for your infinite Love
For having created me in Your image and likeness
For having given You entirely in me

Thank You for your eternal presence in me
For being closer to me than breathing
Near than hands and feet

Thank You Father for your Omnipresence
For your Infinite Presence that fills all spaces
For being the substances of all the cells and organs of my body

Thank You Father for your Omnipotence
For being the only power in the universe
Because in your Presence there are not injustices, poverty, diseases or death

Thank You Father for your Omniscience
For being the only intelligence in the universe
For covering all my needs before asking You

Enlighten me Father!
Open the senses of the Soul to able to see clearly
Help me to make real in my consciousness
Your eternal Presence in me.

PRAYER SUCCESSFULLY ANSWERED

I asked God for strength / To be able to triumph
I was made weak / To humbly learn to obey

I asked for health / To do great things
I was given fragility / To learn to do better things

I asked for riches / To be able to be happy
I was given poverty / To learn to be wise

I asked him for power / To be praised by men
I was given weakness / To learn to feel the need for God

I asked Him for all things / To be able to enjoy life
I was given life / To learn to enjoy all things

I didn't get anything I asked for / But everything I had longed for
In spite of myself / My silent prayers were answered

I am among men / The most richly blessed

(Written by an anonymous Confederate soldier over 150 years ago)

www.ingramcontent.com/pod-product-compliance
Lightning Source LLC
LaVergne TN
LVHW091551060526
838200LV00036B/787